ARTIFICIAL INTELLIGENCE

AI

DR. AJAY KUMAR PHULRE

This book is dedicated to our friends, for the strength they has demonstrated over the last couple of years. It's also dedicated to our family, who always an inspiration to me.

Contents

Foreword   vii

Preface   ix

Acknowledgements   xi

1. Artificial Intelligence   1

2. Problems, State Space Search & Heuristic Search   8
   Techniques

3. Knowledge Representation Issues   53

4. Using Predicate Logic   69

5. Representing Knowledge Using Rules   93

6. Symbolic Reasoning Under Uncertainty   104

7. Statistical Reasoning   115

8. Weak Slot-and-filler Structures   129

9. Strong Slot-and-filler Structures   141

10. Game Playing   151

Foreword

This book is intended to be a pragmatic guide to helping able citizen data scientists to utilize common frameworks and tools to create conversational artificial intelligence experiences for users.

Preface

Artificial Intelligence: Foundations of Computational Agents is a book about the science of artificial intelligence (AI). AI is the study of the design of intelligent computational agents. The book is structured as a textbook but it is designed to be accessible to a wide audience.

Acknowledgements

There are many people whose efforts on this book have contributed to its successful completion. I owe each a debt of gratitude and want to take this opportunity to offer my sincere thanks.

A very special thanks to my publisher, without whose continued interest and support this book would not have been possible. Senior Professor provided support and encouragement when it was most needed. Thanks also to my Marketing Manager of Publisher, whose efforts on this book have been greatly appreciated. Finally, thanks to all the other people at the publishers.

ARTIFICIAL INTELLIGENCE

Artificial Intelligence

- Artificial intelligence is the study of how to make computers do things which, at moment people do better.

- Artificial intelligence can be viewed from a variety of perspectives.

- From the perspective of intelligence, artificial intelligence is making machines "intelligent" -- acting as we would expect people to act. o The inability to distinguish computer responses from human responses is called the Turing test. o Intelligence requires knowledge.

- From a business perspective AI is a set of very powerful tools, and methodologies for using those tools to solve business problems.

- From a programming perspective, AI includes the study of symbolic programming, problem solving, and search.

o Typically AI programs focus on symbols rather than numeric processing. o Problem solving i.e. to achieve a specific goal. o Search - rarely access a solution directly. Search may include a variety of techniques.

• It is the science and engineering of making intelligent machines, especially intelligent computer programs. AI Problems

• Much of the early work in the field of AI focused on formal tasks, such as game playing and theorem proving.

• Game playing and theorem proving share the property that people who do them well are considered to be displaying Intelligence.

• Initially computers could perform well at those tasks simply by being fast at exploring a large number of solution paths and then selecting the best one.

• Humans learn mundane (ordinary) tasks since their birth. They learn by perception, speaking, using language, and training. They learn Formal Tasks and Expert Tasks later.

• Another early foray into AI focused on commonsense reasoning, which includes reasoning about physical objects and their relationship to each other, as well as reasoning about actions and their consequences.

• As AI research progressed, techniques for handling large amount of world knowledge were developed.

• New tasks reasonably attempted such as perception, natural language understanding and problem solving in specialized domains.

• Some of the task domains of artificial intelligence are presented in table I.

• Earlier, all work of AI was concentrated in the mundane task domain.

Mundane tasks	Formal tasks	Expert tasks

Perception
  – Computer Vision
  – Speech, Voice
	Games
	  – Go
	  – Chess (Deep Blue)
	  – Ckeckers
		Engineering
		  – Design
		  – Fault Finding
		  – Manufacturing
		  – Monitoring

Natural Language Processing
  – Understanding
  – Language Generation
  – Language Translation
	Mathematics
	  – Geometry
	  – Logic
	  – Integration and Differentiation
		Scientific Analysis

Common Sense Reasoning	Theorem Proving	Financial Analysis
Planning		Medical Diagnosis
Robot Control		

Table I Task Domains of AI

- Later, it turned out that the machine requires more knowledge, complex knowledge representation, and complicated algorithms for handling mundane tasks.
- This is the reason why AI work is more flourishing in the Expert Tasks domain now, as the expert task domain needs expert knowledge without common sense, which can be easier to represent and handle.

What is an AI technique?

- Artificial intelligence problems span a very broad spectrum. They appear to have very little in common except that they are hard.
- AI Research of earlier decades results into the fact that intelligence requires knowledge.
- Knowledge possess following properties:

- ◦ It is voluminous.
- ◦ It is not well-organized or well-formatted.
- ◦ It is constantly changing.
- ◦ It differs from data. And it is organized in a way that corresponds to its usage.

- AI technique is a method that exploits knowledge that should be represented in such a way that:

  - ◦ Knowledge captures generalization. Situations that share common properties are grouped together. Without this property, inordinate amount of memory and modifications will be required.
  - ◦ It can be understood by people who must provide it. Although bulk of data can be acquired automatically, in many AI domains most of the knowledge must ultimately be provided by people in terms they understand.

  - ◦ It can easily be modified to correct errors and to reflect changes in the world.
  - ◦ It can be used in many situations even though it may not be totally accurate or complete.
  - ◦ It can be used to reduce its own volume by narrowing range of possibilities.

- There are three important AI techniques:

1. Search –

   a. Provides a way of solving problems for which no direct approach is available.

b. It also provides a framework into which any direct techniques that are available can be embedded.

2. Use of knowledge –

a. Provides a way of solving complex problems by exploiting the structure of the objects that are involved.

3. Abstraction –

a. Provides a way of separating important features and variations from many unimportant ones that would otherwise overwhelm any process.

Classification of AI

1. Weak AI: The study and design of machines that perform intelligent tasks.

    ◦ Not concerned with how tasks are performed, mostly concerned with performance and efficiency, such as solutions that are reasonable for NP-Complete problems. E.g., to make a flying machine, use logic and physics, don't mimic a bird.

2. Strong AI: The study and design of machines that simulate the human mind to perform intelligent tasks.

    ◦ Borrow many ideas from psychology, neuroscience. Goal is to perform tasks the way a human might do them – which makes sense, since we do have models of human thought and problem solving.

- Includes psychological ideas in STM, LTM, forgetting, language, genetics, etc. Assumes that the physical symbol hypothesis holds.

3. Evolutionary AI. The study and design of machines that simulate simple creatures, and attempt to evolve and have higher level emergent behavior. For example, ants, bees, etc.

Applications of AI

- AI has been dominant in various fields such as –

1. Gaming – AI plays vital role in strategic games such as chess, poker, tic-tac-toe, etc., where machine can think of large number of possible positions based on heuristic knowledge.
2. Natural Language Processing – It is possible to interact with the computer that

understands natural language spoken by humans.

1. Expert Systems – There are some applications which integrate machine, software, and special information to impart reasoning and advising. They provide explanation and advice to the users.
2. Computer Vision Systems – These systems understand, interpret, and comprehend visual input on the computer.

3. Speech Recognition – Some intelligent systems are capable of hearing and comprehending the language in terms of sentences and their meanings while a human talks to it. It can handle different accents, slang words, noise in the background, change in human's noise, etc.

4. Handwriting Recognition – The handwriting recognition software reads the text written on paper by a pen or on screen by a stylus. It can recognize the shapes of the letters and convert it into editable text.

5. Intelligent Robots – Robots are able to perform the tasks given by a human. They have sensors to detect physical data from the real world such as light, heat, temperature, movement, sound, bump, and pressure. They have efficient processors, multiple sensors and huge memory, to exhibit intelligence. In addition, they are capable of learning from their mistakes and they can adapt to the new environment.

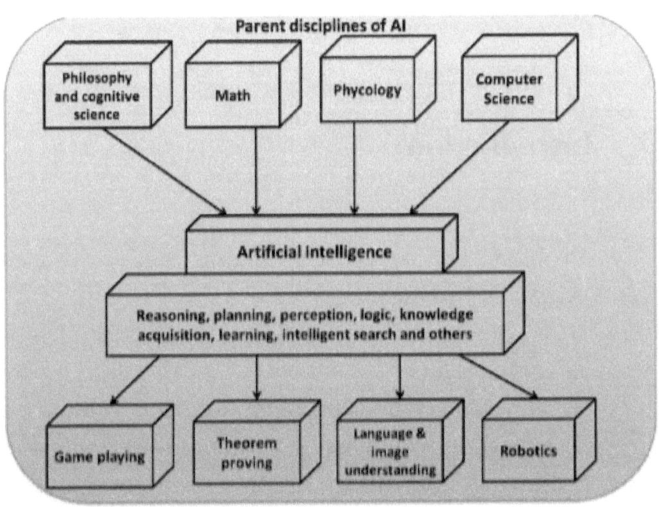

CHAPTER TWO

Problems, State Space Search & Heuristic Search Techniques

Introduction

- Problem solving is the major area of concern in Artificial Intelligence.
- It is the process of generating solution from given observed data.
- To solve a particular problem, we need to build a system or a method which can generate required solution.
- Following four things are required for building such system.

1. Define the problem precisely.

   - This definition must precisely specify the initial situation (input).
   - What final situation (output) will constitute the acceptable solution to the problem.

2. Analyze the problem.

   - To identify those important features which can have an immense impact on the appropriateness of various possible techniques for solving the problem.

3. Isolate and represent the task knowledge that is necessary to solve the problem.
4. Choose the best problem solving technique and apply it to the particular problem.

Defining the Problem as a State Space Search

1. Defining Problem & Search

- A problem is described formally as:

1. Define a state space that contains all the possible configurations of relevant objects.
2. Specify one or more states within that space that describe possible situations from which the problem solving process may start. These states are called initial states.

3. Specify one or more states that would be acceptable as solutions to the problem. These states are called goal states.

4. Specify a set of rules that describe the actions available.

- The problem can then be solved by using the rules, in combination with an appropriate control strategy, to move through the problem space until a path from an initial state to a goal state is found.
- This process is known as search.
- Search is fundamental to the problem-solving process.
- Search is a general mechanism that can be used when more direct method is not known.
- Search also provides the framework into which more direct methods for solving subparts of a problem can be embedded.

1. Defining State & State Space

- A *state* is a representation of problem elements at a given moment.
- *A State space is the set of all states reachable from the initial state.*

  - A state space forms a graph in which the nodes are states and the arcs between nodes are actions.
  - In state space, a path is a sequence of states connected by a sequence of actions.
  - The solution of a problem is part of the graph formed by the state space.

- *The state space representation forms the basis of most of the AI methods.*
- Its structure corresponds to the structure of problem solving in two important ways:

1. It allows for a formal definition of a problem as per the need to convert some given situation into some desired situation using a set of permissible operations.
2. It permits the problem to be solved with the help of known techniques and control strategies to move through the problem space until goal state is found.

3. Define the Problem as State Space Search

Ex.1:- Consider the problem of Playing Chess

- To build a program that could play chess, we have to specify:

  - The starting position of the chess board,
  - The rules that define legal moves, and
  - The board position that represents a win.

- The starting position can be described by an 8 X 8 array square in which each element square (x, y), (x varying from 1 to 8 & y varying from 1 to 8) describes the board position of an appropriate piece in the official chess opening position.
- The goal is any board position in which the opponent does not have a legal move and his

or her "king" is under attack.

- The legal moves provide the way of getting from initial state of final state.
- The legal moves can be described as a set of rules consisting of two parts: A left side that gives the current position and the right side that describes the change to be made to the board position.
- An example is shown in the following figure.

Current Position
While pawn at square (5 , 2), AND Square (5 , 3) is empty, AND Square (5 , 4) is empty.
Changing Board Position
Move pawn from Square (5 , 2) to Square (5 , 4) .

- The current position of a chess coin on the board is **its state** and the set of all possible states is **state space**.
- One or more states where the problem terminates are goal states.
- Chess has approximately 10^{120} game paths. These positions comprise the problem search space.
- Using above formulation, the problem of playing chess is defined as a problem of moving around in a state space, where each state corresponds to a legal position of the

board.

- State space representation seems natural for play chess problem because the set of states, which corresponds to the set of board positions, is well organized.

Ex.2:- Consider Water Jug problem

- A Water Jug Problem: You are given two jugs, a 4-gallon one and a 3-gallon one, a pump which has unlimited water which you can use to fill the jug, and the ground on which water may be poured. Neither jug has any measuring markings on it. How can you get exactly 2 gallons of water in the 4-gallon jug?
- Here the initial state is (0, 0). The goal state is (2, n) for any value of n.
- **State Space Representation:** we will represent a state of the problem as a tuple (x, y) where x represents the amount of water in the 4-gallon jug and y represents the amount of water in the 3-gallon jug. Note that $0 \le x \le 4$, and $0 \le y \le 3$.
- To solve this we have to make some assumptions not mentioned in the problem. They are:

  - We can fill a jug from the pump.
  - We can pour water out of a jug to the ground.
  - We can pour water from one jug to another.
  - There is no measuring device available.

- Operators – we must define a set of operators that will take us from one state to another.

Sr.	Current state	Next State	Descriptions
1	(x, y) if x < 4	(4,y)	Fill the 4 gallon jug
2	(x, y) if y <3	(x,3)	Fill the 3 gallon jug
3	(x, y) if x > 0	(x-d, y)	Pour some water out of the 4 gallon jug
4	(x, y) If y > 0	(x, y-d)	Pour some water out of the 3 gallon jug
5	(x, y) if x>0	(0, y)	Empty the 4 gallon jug
6	(x, y) if y >0	(x,0)	Empty the 3 gallon jug on the ground
7	(x, y) if x+y >= 4 and y > 0	(4, y-(4-x))	Pour water from the 3 gallon jug into the 4 gallon jug until the 4 gallon jug is full
8	(x, y) if x+y >= 3 and x>0	(x-(3-y), 3)	Pour water from the 4 gallon jug into the 3-gallon jug until the 3 gallon jug is full
9	(x, y) if x+y <=4 and y>0	(x+y, 0)	Pour all the water from the 3 gallon jug into the 4 gallon jug

10	(x, y) if x+y <= 3 and x>0	(0, x+y)	Pour all the water from the 4 gallon jug into the 3 gallon jug
11	(0,2)	(2,0)	Pour the 2 gallons from 3 gallon jug into the 4 gallon jug
12	(2,y)	(0,y)	Empty the 2 gallons in the 4 gallon jug on the ground

- There are several sequences of operators that will solve the problem.
- One of the possible solutions is given as:

Gallons in the 4-gallon jug	Gallons in the 3-gallon jug	Rule applied
0	0	2
0	3	9
3	0	2
3	3	7
4	2	5 or 12
0	2	9 Or 11
2	0	--

Ex.3:- Consider 8 puzzle problem

- The 8 puzzle consists of eight numbered, movable tiles set in a 3x3 frame. One cell of the frame is always empty thus making it possible to move an adjacent numbered tile into the empty cell. Such a puzzle is illustrated in following diagram.

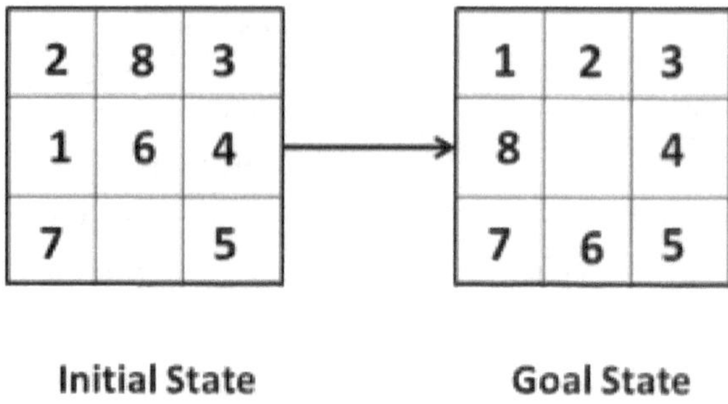

Initial State   Goal State

- The program is to change the initial configuration into the goal configuration.
- A solution to the problem is an appropriate sequence of moves, such as "move tiles 5 to the right, move tile 7 to the left ,move tile 6 to the down" etc...

- To solve a problem, we must specify the global database, the rules, and the control strategy.
- For the 8 puzzle problem that correspond to three components.
- These elements are the problem states, moves and goal.
- In this problem each tile configuration is a state.
- The set of all possible configuration in the problem space, consists of 3,62,880 different configurations of the 8 tiles and blank space.
- For the 8-puzzle, a straight forward description is a 3X3 array of matrix of numbers. Initial global

database is this description of the initial problem state. Virtually any kind of data structure can be used to describe states.

- A move transforms one problem state into another state.

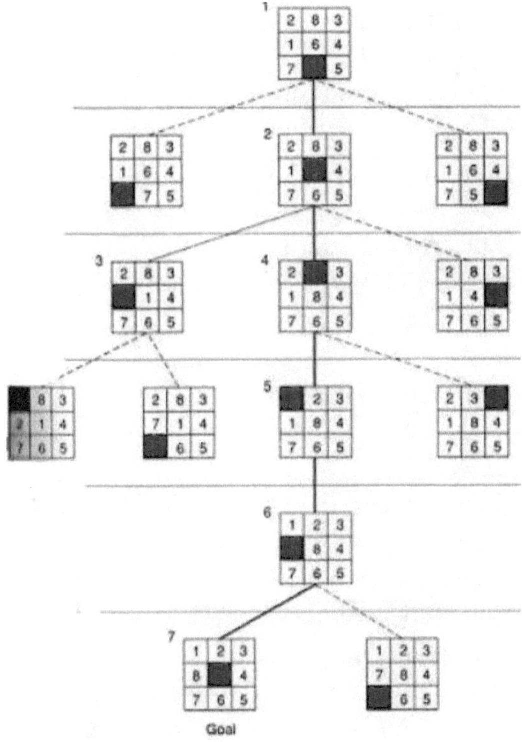

Figure 1: Solution of 8 Puzzle problem

- The 8-puzzle is conveniently interpreted as having the following for moves.

- ◦ Move empty space (blank) to the left, move blank up, move blank to the right and move blank down.
  - ◦ These moves are modeled by production rules that operate on the state descriptions in the appropriate manner.

- The goal condition forms the basis for the termination.
- The control strategy repeatedly applies rules to state descriptions until a description of a goal state is produced.
- It also keeps track of rules that have been applied so that it can compose them into sequence representing the problem solution.
- A solution to the 8-puzzle problem is given in fig. 1.

Production System

- Search process forms the core of many intelligence processes.
- So, it is useful to structure AI programs in a way that facilitates describing and performing the search process.
- Production system provides such structures.
- A production system consists of:

  1. **A set of rules**, each consisting of a left side that determines the applicability of the rule and a right side that describes the operation to be performed if that rule is applied.
  2. **One or more knowledge/databases** that contain whatever information is appropriate for the

particular task. Some parts of the database may be permanent, while other parts of it may pertain only to the solution of the current problem.

3. **A control strategy** that specifies the order in which the rules will be compared to the database and a way of resolving the conflicts that arise when several rules match at once.

4. **A rule applier** which is the computational system that implements the control strategy and applies the rules.

- In order to solve a problem:

○ We must first reduce it to the form for which a precise statement can be given. This can be done by defining the problem's state space (start and goal states) and a set of operators for moving that space.

○ The problem can then be solved by searching for a path through the space from an initial state to a goal state.

○ The process of solving the problem can usefully be modeled as a production system.

Benefits of Production System

1. Production systems provide an excellent tool for structuring AI programs.

2. Production Systems are highly modular because the individual rules can be added, removed or modified independently.

3. The production rules are expressed in a natural form, so the statements contained in the

knowledge base should be easily understandable.

Production System Characteristics

1. Monotonic Production System: the application of a rule never prevents the later application of another rule that could also have been applied at the time the first rule was selected. i.e., rules are independent.
2. Non-Monotonic Production system is one in which this is not true.
3. Partially commutative Production system: a production system with the property that if application of a particular sequence of rules transforms state x to state y, then allowable permutation of those rules, also transforms state x into state y.
4. Commutative Production system: A Commutative production system is a production system that is both monotonic and partially commutative.

Control Strategies

- Control strategies help us decide which rule to apply next during the process of searching for a solution to a problem.
- Good control strategy should:

  1. It should cause motion
  2. It should be Systematic

- Control strategies are classified as:

1. Uninformed/blind search control strategy:

- ○ Do not have additional information about states beyond problem definition.
- ○ Total search space is looked for solution.
- ○ Example: Breadth First Search (BFS), Depth First Search (DFS), Depth Limited Search (DLS).

2. Informed/Directed Search Control Strategy:

- ○ Some information about problem space is used to compute preference among the various possibilities for exploration and expansion.
- ○ Examples: Best First Search, Problem Decomposition, A*, Mean end Analysis

Breadth-First Search Strategy (BFS)

- This is an exhaustive search technique.
- The search generates all nodes at a particular level before proceeding to the next level of the tree.
- *The search systematically proceeds testing each node that is reachable from a parent node before it expands to any child of those nodes.*
- Search terminates when a solution is found and the test returns true.

Algorithm:

1. *Create a variable called NODE-LIST and set it to initial state.*
2. *Until a goal state is found or NODE-LIST is empty do:*

i. *Remove the first element from NODE-LIST and call it E. If NODE-LIST was empty, quit.*

ii. *For each way that each rule can match the state described in E do:*

    a. *Apply the rule to generate a new state.*

    b. *If the new state is a goal state, quit and return this state.*

    c. *Otherwise, add the new state to the end of NODE-LIST.*

Depth-First Search Strategy (DFS)

- Here, the search systematically proceeds to some depth *d*, before another path is considered.
- If the maximum depth of search tree is reached and if the solution has not been found, then the search backtracks to the previous level and explores any remaining alternatives at this level, and so on.

Algorithm:

1. *If the initial state is a goal state, quit and return success*
2. *Otherwise, do the following until success or failure is signaled:*

    a. *Generate a successor, E, of initial state. If there are no more successors, signal failure.*

    b. *Call Depth-First Search, with E as the initial state*

    c. *If success is returned, signal success. Otherwise continue in this loop.*

Comparison: DFS & BFS

Depth First Search	Breath First Search
DFS requires less memory since only the nodes on the current path are stored.	BFS guarantees that the space of possible moves is systematically examined; this search requires considerable memory resources.
By chance, DFS may find a solution without examining much of the search space at all. Then it finds solution faster.	The search systematically proceeds testing each node that is reachable from a parent node before it expands to any child of those nodes.
If the selected path does not reach to the solution node, DFS gets stuck into a blind alley.	BFS will not get trapped exploring a blind alley.
Does not guarantee to find solution. Backtracking is required if wrong path is selected.	If there is a solution, BFS is guaranteed to find it.

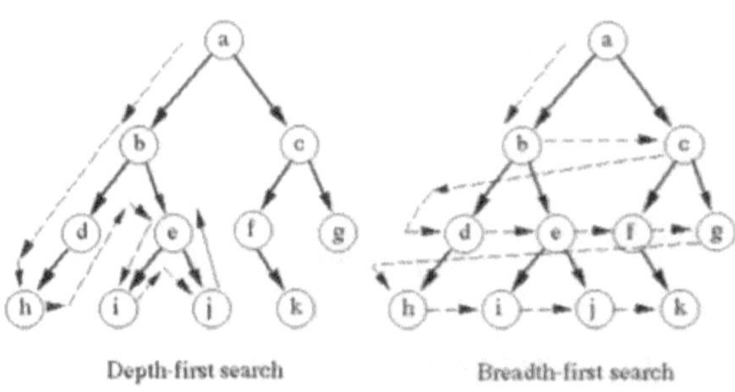

Depth-first search　　　　Breadth-first search

Iterative Deepening Search

- Depth first search is incomplete if there is an infinite branch in the search tree.

- Infinite branches can happen if:

  ◦ paths contain loops
  ◦ infinite number of states and/or operators.

- For problems with infinite (or just very large) state spaces, several variants of depth-first search have been developed:

  ◦ depth limited search
  ◦ iterative deepening search

- Depth limited search (DLS) is a form of depth-first search.
- It expands the search tree depth-first up to a maximum depth ?
- The nodes at depth ? are treated as if they had no successors
- If the search reaches a node at depth ? where the path is not a solution, we backtrack to the next choice point at $????h < ?$
- Depth-first search can be viewed as a special case of DLS with ? = ∞
- The depth bound can sometimes be chosen based on knowledge of the problem
- For e.g., in the route planning problem, the longest route has length ? − 1, where ? is the number of cities (states), so we can set ? = ? − 1
- For the most problems, ? is unknown.
- Iterative deepening (depth-first) search (IDS) is a form of depth limited search which progressively increases the bound.

- It first tries ? = 1, then ? = 2, then ? = 3, etc. until a solution is found
- Solution will be found when ? = ?
- IDDFS combines depth-first search's space-efficiency and breadth-first search's fast search

(for nodes closer to root).

- IDDFS calls DFS for different depths starting from an initial value. In every call, DFS is restricted from going beyond given depth. So basically we do DFS in a BFS fashion.
- The example of Iterative-deepening depth-first search as given below, with the current depth-limit (?) starting at 1 and incrementing each time:

Iterative Deepening Search

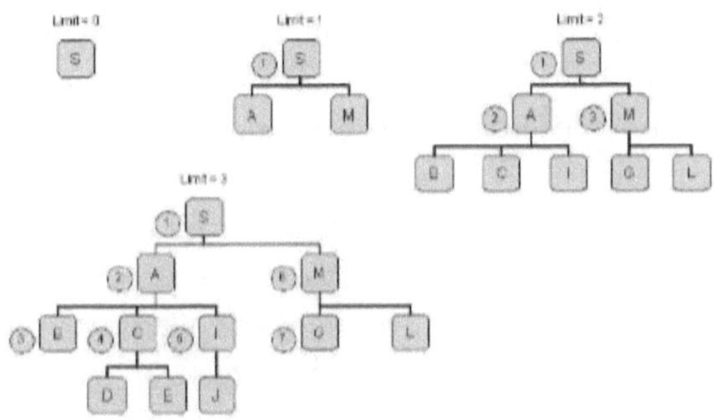

Problem Characteristics

- In order to choose the most appropriate problem solving method, it is necessary to analyze the problem along various key dimensions.
- These dimensions are referred to as problem characteristics discussed below.

1. Is the problem decomposable into a set of independent smaller or easier sub-problems?

   - A very large and composite problem can be easily solved if it can be broken into smaller problems and recursion could be used.
   - For example, we want to solve :- $\int$?2 + 3? + ???2? ????2? ??
   - This can be done by breaking it into three smaller problems and solving each by applying specific rules. Adding the results we can find the complete solution.
   - But there are certain problems which cannot be decomposed into sub-problems.

     - Here, solution can be achieved be moving blocks in a sequence such that goal state can be derived.
     - Solution steps are interdependent and cannot be decomposed in sub problems.
     - These two examples, symbolic integration and the blocks world illustrate the difference between decomposable and non-decomposable problems.

   - Can solution steps be ignored or at least undone if they prove unwise?

- Problem fall under three classes, (i) ignorable, (ii) recoverable and (iii) irrecoverable.

- This classification is with reference to the steps of the solution to a problem.
- Consider theorem proving. We may later find that it is of no use. We can still proceed further, since nothing is lost by this redundant step. This is an example of ignorable solutions steps.
- Now consider the 8 puzzle problem tray and arranged in specified order.
- While moving from the start state towards goal state, we may make some stupid move but we can backtrack and undo the unwanted move. This only involves additional steps and the solution steps are recoverable.
- Lastly consider the game of chess. If a wrong move is made, it can neither be ignored nor be recovered. The thing to do is to make the best use of current situation and proceed. This is an example of an irrecoverable solution steps.
- Knowledge of these will help in determining the control structure.

  - Ignorable problems can be solved using a simple control structure that never backtracks.
  - Recoverable problems can be solved by a slightly more complicated control strategy that allows backtracking.
  - Irrecoverable problems will need to be solved by a system that expends a great deal of effort making each decision since decision must be final.

- Is the problem's universe predictable?

  - Problems can be classified into those with certain outcome (eight puzzle and water jug problems) and those with uncertain outcome (playing cards).
  - In certain – outcome problems, planning could be done to generate a sequence of operators that guarantees to lead to a solution.
  - Planning helps to avoid unwanted solution steps.
  - For uncertain outcome problems, planning can at best generate a sequence of operators that has a good probability of leading to a solution.
  - The uncertain outcome problems do not guarantee a solution and it is often very expensive since the number of solution paths to be explored increases exponentially with the number of points at which the outcome cannot be predicted.
  - Thus one of the hardest types of problems to solve is the irrecoverable, uncertain –

- outcome problems (Ex:- Playing cards).
- Is a good solution to the problem obvious without comparison to all other possible solutions?

  - There are two categories of problems - Any path problem and Best path problem.
  - In any path problem, like the water jug and 8 puzzle problems, we are satisfied with the solution, irrespective of the solution path taken.
  - Whereas in the other category not just any solution is acceptable but we want the best path solution.

- Like that of traveling sales man problem, which is the shortest path problem.
- In any – path problems, by heuristic methods we obtain a solution and we do not

○ explore alternatives.

- Any path problems can often be solved in a reasonable amount of time by using heuristics that suggest good paths to explore.
- For the best-path problems all possible paths are explored using an exhaustive search until the best path is obtained.
- Best path problems are computationally harder.

○ Is the desired solution a state of the world or a path to a state?

- Consider the problem of natural language processing.
- Finding a consistent interpretation for the sentence "The bank president ate a dish of pasta salad with the fork".
- We need to find the interpretation but not the record of the processing by which the interpretation is found.
- Contrast this with the water jug problem.
- In water jug problem, it is not sufficient to report that we have solved, but the path that we found to the state (2, 0). Thus the statement of a solution to this problem must be a sequence of operations that produces the final state.

- What is the role of knowledge?

  - Though one could have unlimited computing power, the size of the knowledge base available for solving the problem does matter in arriving at a good solution.
  - Take for example the game of playing chess, just the rules for determining legal moves and some simple control mechanism is sufficient to arrive at a solution.
  - But additional knowledge about good strategy and tactics could help to constrain the search and speed up the execution of the program. The solution would then be realistic.
  - Consider the case of predicting the political trend. This would require an enormous amount of knowledge even to be able to recognize a solution, leave alone the best.

- Does the task require interaction with a person?
- The problems can again be categorized under two heads.
- Solitary in which the computer will be given a problem description and will produce an answer, with no intermediate communication and with the demand for an explanation of the reasoning process. Simple theorem proving falls under this category. Given the basic rules and laws, the theorem could be proved, if one exists.
- Conversational, in which there will be intermediate communication between a person and the computer, either to provide additional assistance to the computer or to provide additional information to the

user, or both, such as medical diagnosis fall under this category, where people will be unwilling to accept the verdict of the program, if they cannot follow its reasoning.

- Problem Classification

    - Actual problems are examined from the point of view of all these questions; it becomes apparent that there are several broad classes into which the problems fall.

    -

Issues in the design of search programs

- The direction in which to conduct the search (forward versus backward reasoning). If the search proceeds from start state towards a goal state, it is a forward search or we can also search from the goal.
- How to select applicable rules (Matching). Production systems typically spend most of their time looking for rules to apply. So, it is critical to have efficient procedures for matching rules against states.
- How to represent each node of the search process (knowledge representation problem).

-

Heuristic Search Techniques

    - In order to solve many hard problems efficiently, it is often necessary to compromise the requirements of mobility and systematicity and to construct a control structure that is no longer guaranteed to find the best answer but will always find a very good answer.

- Usually very hard problems tend to have very large search spaces. Heuristics can be used to limit search process.
- There are good general purpose heuristics that are useful in a wide variety of problem domains.
- Special purpose heuristics exploit domain specific knowledge.
- For example nearest neighbor heuristics for shortest path problem. It works by selecting locally superior alternative at each step.
- Applying nearest neighbor heuristics to Travelling Salesman Problem:

1. Arbitrarily select a starting city
2. To select the next city, look at all cities not yet visited and select the one closest to the current city. Go to next step.
3. Repeat step 2 until all cities have been visited.

- This procedure executes in time proportional to N^2, where N is the number of cities to be visited.

o

Heuristic Function

- *Heuristic function maps from problem state descriptions to measures of desirability, usually represented as numbers.*
- Which aspects of the problem state are considered, how those aspects are evaluated, and

the weights given to individual aspects are chosen in such a way that the value of the heuristic function at a given node in the search process gives as good an estimate as possible of whether that node is on the desired path to a solution.

- Well-designed heuristic functions can play an important part in efficiently guiding a search process toward a solution.
- Every search process can be viewed as a traversal of a directed graph, in which the nodes represent problem states and the arcs represent relationships between states.

- The search process must find a path through this graph, starting at an initial state and ending in one or more final states.
- Domain-specific knowledge must be added to improve search efficiency. Information about the problem includes the nature of states, cost of transforming from one state to another, and characteristics of the goals.
- This information can often be expressed in the form of heuristic evaluation function.
- In general, heuristic search improve the quality of the path that are exported.
- Using good heuristics we can hope to get good solutions to hard problems such as the traveling salesman problem in less than exponential time.

Heuristic Search Techniques

- Generate-and-Test

- Generate-and-test search algorithm is a very simple algorithm that guarantees to find a solution if done systematically and there exists a solution.

○ Algorithm:

○ *Generate a possible solution. For some problems, this means generating a particular point in the problem space. For others it means generating a path from a start stat.*

○ *Test to see if this is actually a solution by comparing the chosen point or the endpoint of the chosen path to the set of acceptable goal states.*

○ *If a solution has been found, quit, Otherwise return to step 1.*

- It is a depth first search procedure since complete solutions must be generated before they can be tested.
- In its most systematic form, it is simply an exhaustive search of the problem space.

○ - It operates by generating solutions randomly.

○ Simple Hill Climbing

- Hill climbing is a variant of generate-and test in which feedback from the test procedure is used to help the generator decide which direction to move in search space.
- The test function is augmented with a heuristic function that provides an estimate of how close a given state is to the goal state.

- Hill climbing is often used when a good heuristic function is available for evaluating states but when no other useful knowledge is available.
- ***The key difference between Simple Hill climbing and Generate-and-test is the use of evaluation function as a way to inject task specific knowledge into the control process.***

- **Algorithm:**
- *Evaluate the initial state. If it is also goal state, then return it and quit. Otherwise continue with the initial state as the current state.*
- *Loop until a solution is found or until there are no new operators left to be applied in the current state:*

  a. *Select an operator that has not yet been applied to the current state and*

  - *apply it to produce a new state.*

  b. *Evaluate the new state*

     i. *If it is the goal state, then return it and quit.*
     ii. *If it is not a goal state but it is better than the current state, then make it the current state.*
     iii. *If it is not better than the current state, then continue in the loop.*

- Steepest-Ascent Hill Climbing

  - This is a variation of simple hill climbing which considers all the moves from the current state and selects the best one as the next state.

- At each current state we select a transition, evaluate the resulting state, and if the resulting state is an improvement we move there, otherwise we try a new transition from where we were.
- We repeat this until we reach a goal state, or have no more transitions to try.
- The transitions explored can be selected at random, or according to some problem specific heuristics.

○ Algorithm

○ *Evaluate the initial state. If it is also a goal state, then return it and quit. Otherwise, continue with the initial state as the current state.*

○ *Loop until a solution is found or until a complete iteration produces no change to current state:*

a. *Let S be a state such that any possible successor of the current state will be better than S.*

b. *For each operator that applies to the current state do:*

    i. *Apply the operator and generate a new state*

    ii. *Evaluate the new state. If is is a goal state, then return it and quit. If not, compare it to S. If it is better, then set S to this state. If it is not better, leave S alone.*

c. *If the S is better than the current state, then set current state to S.*

- Hill Climbing has three well-known drawbacks:

- **Local Maxima**: a local maximum is a state that is better than all its neighbors but is not better than some other states further away.
- **Plateau**: a plateau is a flat area of the search space in which, a whole set of neighboring states have the same values.
- **Ridge**: is a special kind of local maximum. It is an area of the search space that is higher than surrounding areas and that itself has slop.

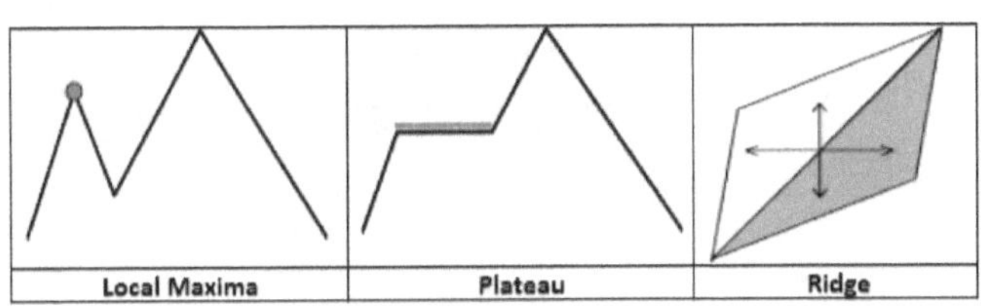

- In each of the previous cases (local maxima, plateaus & ridge), the algorithm reaches a point at which no progress is being made.
- A solution is,

i. Backtrack to some earlier node and try going in a different direction.
ii. Make a big jump to try to get in a new section.
iii. Moving in several directions at once.

- Simulated Annealing (SA)

  - Motivated by the physical annealing process.

- Material is heated and slowly cooled into a uniform structure. Simulated annealing mimics this process.
- Compared to hill climbing the main difference is that SA allows downwards steps.
- Simulated annealing also differs from hill climbing in that a move is selected at random and then decides whether to accept it.
- *To accept or not to accept?*

  - The law of thermodynamics states that at temperature, t, the probability of an increase in energy of magnitude, ??, is given by,

    - $?(??) = ???(-?? \, / ??)$

  - Where k is a constant known as Boltzmann's constant and it is incorporated into T.
  - So the revised probability formula is,

    - $?'(??) = ???(-?? \, / ?)$

  - ?? is the positive change in the objective function and T is the current temperature.
  - The probability of accepting a worse state is a function of both the temperature of the system and the change in the cost function.
  - As the temperature decreases, the probability of accepting worse moves decreases.
  - If t=0, no worse moves are accepted (i.e. hill climbing).

- Algorithm

- *Evaluate the initial state. If it is also a goal state, then return it and quit. Otherwise, continue with the initial state as the current state.*
- Initialize BEST-SO-FAR to the current state.
- Initialize T according to the annealing schedule.
- Loop until a solution is found or until there are no new operators left to be applied in the
-     current state.

  a. Select an operator that has not yet been applied to the current state and apply it to produce a new state.
  b. Evaluate the new state. Compute

- ?? = (value of current) − (value of new state)

  - If the new state is a goal state, then return it and quit.
  - If it is not a goal state but is better than the current state, then make it the current state. Also set BEST-SO-FAR to this new state.
  - If it is not better than the current state, then make it the current state with probability ?' as defined above. This step is usually implemented by generating a random number between [0, 1]. If the number is less than

- ?', then the move is accepted otherwise do nothing.

  c. Revise T as necessary according to the annealing
-     schedule.

- Best First Search

- DFS is good because it allows a solution to be found without expanding all competing branches. BFS is good because it does not get trapped on dead end paths.
- Best first search combines the advantages of both DFS and BFS into a single method.
- One way of combining BFS and DFS is to follow a single path at a time, but switch paths whenever some competing path looks more promising than the current one does.
- At each step of the Best First Search process; we select the most promising of the nodes we have generated so far.
- This is done by applying an appropriate heuristic function to each of them.
- We then expand the chosen node by using the rules to generate its successors.
- If one of them is a solution, we can quit. If not, all those new nodes are added to the set of nodes generated so far.

- **<u>OR Graphs</u>**

- It is sometimes important to search graphs so that duplicate paths will not be pursued.
- An algorithm to do this will operate by searching a directed graph in which each node represents a point in problem space.
- Each node will contain:

  - Description of problem state it represents
  - Indication of how promising it is

- ○ Parent link that points back to the best node from which it came
- ○ List of nodes that were generated from it

- Parent link will make it possible to recover the path to the goal, once the goal is found.
- The list of successors will make it possible, if a better path is found to an already existing node, to propagate the improvement down to its successors.
- This is called OR-graph, since each of its branches represents an alternative problem solving

○ OPEN – nodes that have been generated and have had the heuristic function applied to them but which have not yet been examined. OPEN is actually a priority queue in which the elements with the highest priority are those with the most promising value of the heuristic function.

○ CLOSED- nodes that have already been examined. We need to keep these nodes in memory if we want to search a graph rather than a tree, since whenever a new node is generated; we need to check whether it has been generated before.

○ Algorithm: Best First Search

○ *Start with OPEN containing just the initial state*

○ *Until a goal is found or there are no nodes left on OPEN do:*

a. *Pick the best node on OPEN*

b. *Generate its successors*

c. *For each successor do:*

   i.   *If it has not been generated before, evaluate it, add it to OPEN, and record its parent.*

   ii.   *If it has been generated before, change the parent if this new path is better than the previous one. In that case, update the cost of getting to this node and to any successors that this node may already have.*

Best First Search example

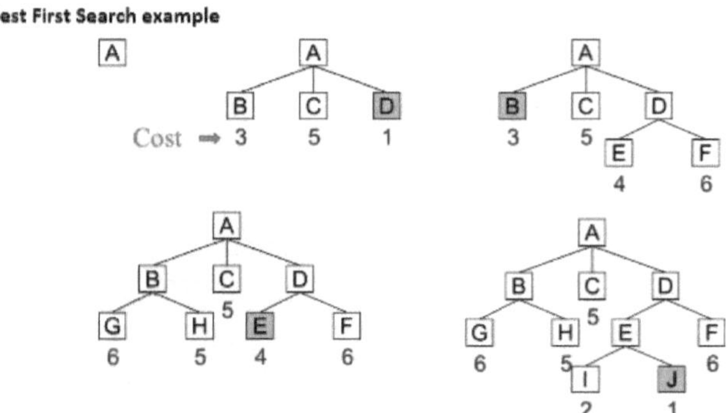

The A* Algorithm

- Best First Search is a simplification of A* Algorithm.
- This algorithm uses following functions:

1. *f'*: Heuristic function that estimates the merits of each node we generate. $f' = g + h'$. *f'* represents an estimate of the cost of getting from the initial state to a goal state along with the path that generated the current node.
2. *g:* The function *g* is a measure of the cost of getting from initial state to the current node.

3. **h'**: The function *h'* is an estimate of the additional cost of getting from the current node to a goal state.

- The algorithm also uses the lists: OPEN and CLOSED

Algorithm: A*

1. *Start with OPEN containing only initial node. Set that node's g value to 0, its h' value to whatever it is, and its f' value to h'+0 or h'. Set CLOSED to empty list.*
2. *Until a goal node is found, repeat the following procedure: If there are no nodes on OPEN, report failure. Otherwise select the node on OPEN with the lowest f' value. Call it BESTNODE. Remove it from OPEN. Place it in CLOSED. See if the BESTNODE is a goal state. If so exit and report a solution. Otherwise, generate the successors of BESTNODE but do not set the BESTNODE to point to them yet. For each of the SUCCESSOR, do the following:*

   a. *Set SUCCESSOR to point back to BESTNODE. These backwards links will make it possible to recover the path once a solution is found.*
   b. *Compute g(SUCCESSOR) = g(BESTNODE) + the cost of getting from BESTNODE to SUCCESSOR*
   c. *See if SUCCESSOR is the same as any node on OPEN. If so call the node OLD.*

      i. *Check whether it is cheaper to get to OLD via its current parent or to SUCESSOR via BESTNODE by comparing their g values.*
      ii. *If OLD is cheaper, then do nothing. If SUCCESSOR is cheaper then reset*

OLD's parent link to point to BESTNODE.

   iii. *Record the new cheaper path in g(OLD) and update f '(OLD).*

b. *If SUCCESSOR was not on OPEN, see if it is on CLOSED. If so, call the node on CLOSED OLD and add OLD to the list of BESTNODE's successors.*
c. *If SUCCESSOR was not already on either OPEN or CLOSED, then put it on OPEN and add it to the list of BESTNODE's successors. Compute f'(SUCCESSOR) = g(SUCCESSOR) + h'(SUCCESSOR).*

Observations about A*

- Role of g function: This lets us choose which node to expand next on the basis of not only of how good the node itself looks, but also on the basis of how good the path to the node was.
- h', the distance of a node to the goal. If h' is a perfect estimator of h, then A* will converge immediately to the goal with no search.

Admissibility of A*

- A heuristic function h'(n) is said to be admissible if it never overestimates the cost of

getting to a goal state.

- i.e. if the true minimum cost of getting from node n to a goal state is C then h must satisfy: $h'(n) \leq C$

- ○ If h' is a perfect estimator of h, then A* will converge immediately to the goal state with no search.
- ○ If h' never overestimates h, then A* algorithm is guaranteed to find an optimal path if one exists.

II. Problem Reduction

AND-OR graphs

- ○ AND-OR graph (or tree) is useful for representing the solution of problems that can be solved by decomposing them into a set of smaller problems, all of which must then be solved.
- ○ This decomposition or reduction generates arcs that we call AND arcs.
- ○ One AND arc may point to any numbers of successor nodes. All of which must then be solved in order for the arc to point solution.
- ○ In order to find solution in an AND-OR graph we need an algorithm similar to best –first search but with the ability to handle the AND arcs appropriately.
- ○ *We define FUTILITY, if the estimated cst of solution becomes greater than the value f FUTILITY then we abandon the search, FUTILITY should be chosen to crrespond to a threshld.*
- ○ The AO* Algorithm

  - • Rather than the two lists, OPEN and CLOSED, that were used in the A* algorithm, the AO* algorithm will use a single structure GRAPH, representing the part of the search graph that has been explicitly generated so far.

- Each node in the graph will point both down to its immediate successors and up to its immediate predecessors.
- Each node in the graph will also have associated with it an h' value, an estimate of the cost of a path from itself to a set of solution nodes.
- We will not store g (the cost of getting from the start node to the current node) as we did in the A* algorithm.
- And such a value is not necessary because of the top-down traversing of the edge

○ which guarantees that only nodes that are on the best path will ever be considered for expansion.

Algorithm: AO*

○ Let GRAPH consist only of the node representing the initial state. Call this node INIT, Compute VINIT.

○ Until INIT is labeled SOLVED or until INIT's h' value becomes greater than FUTILITY, repeat the following procedure:

a. Trace the labeled arcs from INIT and select for expansion one of the as yet unexpanded nodes that occurs on this path. Call the selected node NODE.

b. Generate the successors of NODE. If there are none, then assign FUTILITY as the h' value of NODE. This is equivalent to saying that NODE is not solvable. If there are successors, then for each one (called SUCCESSOR) that is not also an ancestor of NODE do the following:

   i. Add SUCCESSOR to GRAPH

   ii. If SUCCESSOR is a terminal node, label it SOLVED and assign it an h' value of 0

  iii. If SUCCESSOR is not a terminal node, compute its h' value

c. Propagate the newly discovered information up the graph by doing the following: Let S be a set of nodes that have been labeled SOLVED or whose h' values have been changed and so need to have values propagated back to their parents. Initialize S to NODE. Until S is empty, repeat the, following procedure:

   i. If possible, select from S a node none of whose descendants in GRAPH occurs in S. If there is no such node, select any node from S. Call this node CURRENT, and remove it from S.

  ii. Compute the cost of each of the arcs emerging from CURRENT. The cost of each arc is equal to the sum of the h' values of each of the nodes at the end of the arc plus whatever the cost of the arc itself is. Assign as CURRENT'S new h' value the minimum of the costs just computed for the arcs emerging from it.

  iii. Mark the best path out of CURRENT by marking the arc that had the minimum cost as computed in the previous step.

  iv. Mark CURRENT SOLVED if all of the nodes connected to it through the new labeled arc have been labeled SOLVED.

  v. If CURRENT has been labeled SOLVED or if the cost of CURRENT was just changed, then its new status must be propagated back up the graph. So

- ◦   add all of the ancestors of CURRENT to S.

- ◦ Constraint Satisfaction

  - Constraint satisfaction is a search procedure that operates in a space of constraint sets. The

- ◦ initial state contains the constraints that are originally given in the problem description.

  - A goal state is any state that has been constrained "enough" where "enough" must be defined for each problem.
  - For example, in cryptarithmetic problems, enough means that each letter has been assigned a unique numeric value.
  - Constraint Satisfaction problems in AI have goal of discovering some problem state that satisfies a given set of constraints.
  - Design tasks can be viewed as constraint satisfaction problems in which a design must be created within fixed limits on time, cost, and materials.
  - Constraint Satisfaction is a two-step process:

- ◦ First constraints are discovered and propagated as far as possible throughout the system.
- ◦ Then if there is still not a solution, search begins. A guess about something is made and added as a new constraint.
- ◦ **<u>Example: Cryptarithmetic Problem</u>**
  Constraints:
- ◦ No two letters have the same value

- The sums of the digits must be as shown in the problem Goal State:

- All letters have been assigned a digit in such a way that all the initial constraints are satisfied

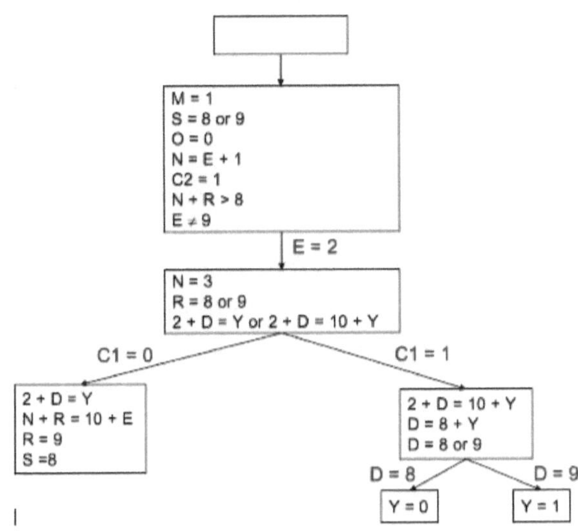

- The solution process proceeds in cycles. At each cycle, two significant things are done:

- Constraints are propagated by using rules that correspond to the properties of arithmetic.
- A value is guessed for some letter whose value is not yet determined.

-

Solution:

Algorithm: Constraint Satisfaction

- *Propagate available constraints. To do this first set OPEN to set of all objects that must have values assigned to them in a complete solution. Then do until an inconsistency is detected or until OPEN is empty:*

  a. *Select an object OB from OPEN. Strengthen as much as possible the set of constraints that apply to OB.*
  b. *If this set is different from the set that was assigned the last time OB was examined or if this is the first time OB has been examined, then add to OPEN all objects that share any constraints with OB.*
  c. *Remove OB from OPEN.*

- *If the union of the constraints discovered above defines a solution, then quit and report the solution.*
- *If the union of the constraints discovered above defines a contradiction, then return the*
-    *failure.*
- *If neither of the above occurs, then it is necessary to make a guess at something in order to proceed. To do this loop until a solution is found or all possible solutions have been eliminated:*

  a. *Select an object whose value is not yet determined and select a way of strengthening the constraints on that object.*

b. *Recursively invoke constraint satisfaction with the current set of constraints augmented by strengthening constraint just selected.*

- Means-Ends Analysis

  - Collection of strategies presented so far can reason either forward or backward, but for a given problem, one direction or the other must be chosen.
  - A mixture of the two directions is appropriate. Such a mixed strategy would make it possible to solve the major parts of a problem first and then go back and solve the small problems that arise in "gluing" the big pieces together.
  - The technique of Means-Ends Analysis (MEA) allows us to do that.
  - MEA process centers around the detection of differences between the current state and the goal state.
  - Once such a difference is isolated, an operator that can reduce the difference must be found.
  - If the operator cannot be applied to the current state, we set up a sub-problem of getting to a state in which it can be applied.
  - The kind of backward chaining in which operators are selected and then sub-goals are set up to establish the preconditions of the operators is called operator sub-goaling

- Algorithm: Means-Ends Analysis
- *Compare CURRENT to GOAL. If there are no differences between them then return.*

○ *Otherwise, select the most important difference and reduce it by doing the following until success or failure is signaled:*

   a. *Select an as yet untried operator O that is applicable to the current difference. If there are no such operators, then signal failure.*

   b. *Attempt to apply O to CURRENT. Generate descriptions of two states: O- START, a state in which O's preconditions are satisfied and O-RESULT, the state that would result if O were applied in O-START.*

   c. *If*

○ *(LAST-PART ß MEA(O-RESULT, GOAL))*

are successful, then signal success and return the result of concatenating FIRST-PART, O, and LAST-PART.

and

(FIRST-PARTß MEA(CURRENT, O-START))

CHAPTER THREE

Knowledge Representation Issues

Representations and Mappings

- In order to solve complex problems encountered in artificial intelligence, one needs both a large amount of knowledge and some mechanism for manipulating that knowledge to create solutions.
- Knowledge and Representation are two distinct entities. They play central but distinguishable roles in intelligent system.
- *Knowledge is a description of the world. It determines a system's competence by what it knows.*
- **Representation is the way knowledge is encoded. It defines a system's performance in doing something.**
- Different types of knowledge require different kinds of representation.

- The Knowledge Representation models/mechanisms are often based on:

  ◦ Logic
  ◦ Rules
  ◦ Frames
  ◦ Semantic Net

- Knowledge is categorized into two major types:

1. Tacit corresponds to "informal" or "implicit"

   ◦ Exists within a human being;
   ◦ It is embodied.
   ◦ Difficult to articulate formally.
   ◦ Difficult to communicate or share.
   ◦ Hard to steal or copy.
   ◦ Drawn from experience, action, subjective insight

2. Explicit formal type of knowledge, Explicit

   ◦ Explicit knowledge
   ◦ Exists outside a human being;
   ◦ It is embedded.
   ◦ Can be articulated formally.
   ◦ Can be shared, copied, processed and stored.
   ◦ Easy to steal or copy
   ◦ Drawn from artifact of some type as principle, procedure, process, concepts.

- A variety of ways of representing knowledge have been exploited in AI programs.

- There are two different kinds of entities, we are dealing with.

1. Facts: Truth in some relevant world. Things we want to represent.
2. Representation of facts in some chosen formalism. Things we will actually be able to manipulate.

- These entities are structured at two levels:

1. The knowledge level, at which facts are described.
2. The symbol level, at which representation of objects are defined in terms of symbols that can be manipulated by programs.

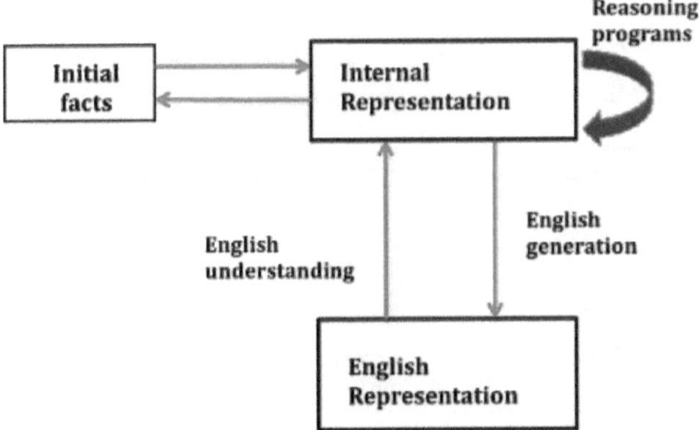

Fig. 3.1 Mapping between Facts and Representations

Framework of Knowledge Representation

- Computer requires a well-defined problem description to process and provide well-defined acceptable solution.
- To collect fragments of knowledge we need first to formulate a description in our spoken language and then represent it in formal language so that computer can understand.
- The computer can then use an algorithm to compute an answer. This process is illustrated as,

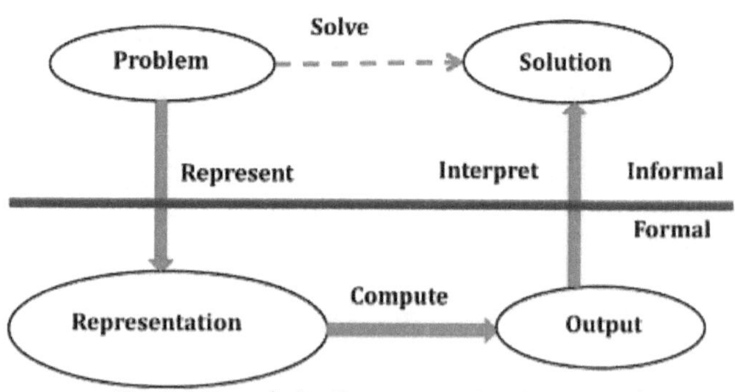

Fig. 3.2 Knowledge Representation Framework

- The steps are:

○ The informal formalism of the problem takes place first.
○ It is then represented formally and the computer produces an output.

○ This output can then be represented in an informally described solution that user understands or checks for consistency.

- The Problem solving requires,

◦ Formal knowledge representation, and
◦ Conversion of informal knowledge to formal knowledge that is conversion of implicit knowledge to explicit knowledge.

Mapping between Facts and Representation

- Knowledge is a collection of facts from some domain.
- We need a representation of "facts" that can be manipulated by a program.
- Normal English is insufficient, too hard currently for a computer program to draw inferences in natural languages.

Thus some symbolic representation is necessary.

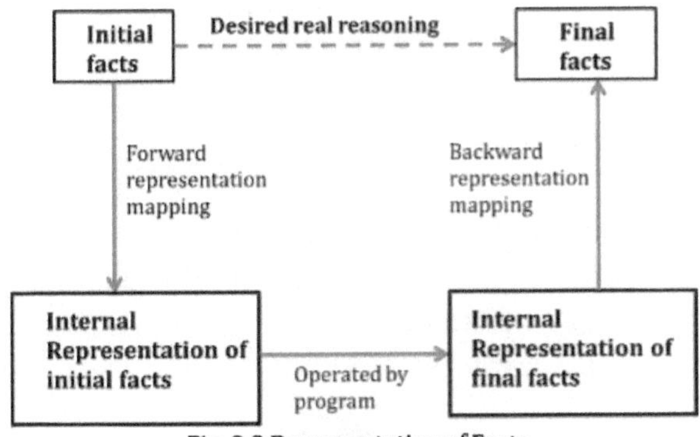

Fig. 3.3 Representation of Facts

Enter Caption

Approaches to knowledge Representation

- A good knowledge representation enables fast and accurate access to knowledge and understanding of the content.
- A knowledge representation system should have following properties.

1. Representational Adequacy

   - The ability to represent all kinds of knowledge that are needed in that domain.

2. Inferential Adequacy

   - The ability to manipulate the representational structures to derive new structures corresponding to new knowledge inferred from old.

3. Inferential Efficiency

   - The ability to incorporate additional information into the knowledge structure that can be used to focus the attention of the inference mechanisms in the most

     promising direction.

     1. Acquisitional Efficiency

- ○ The ability to acquire new knowledge using automatic methods wherever possible rather than reliance on human intervention.

Knowledge Representation Schemes

1. **Relational Knowledge :**

   - ○ The simplest way to represent declarative facts is as a set of relations of the same sort used in the database system.
   - ○ Provides a framework to compare two objects based on equivalent attributes.
   - ○ Any instance in which two different objects are compared is a relational type of knowledge.
   - ○ The table below shows a simple way to store facts.

     - ▪ The facts about a set of objects are put systematically in columns.

This representation provides little opportunity for inference.

Player	Height	Weight	Bats - Throws
Aaron	6-0	180	Right - Right
Mays	5-10	170	Right - Right
Ruth	6-2	215	Left - Left
Williams	6-3	205	Left - Right

- ▪ Given the facts it is not possible to answer simple question such as :

"Who is the heaviest player?"

- But if a procedure for finding heaviest player is provided, then these facts will enable that procedure to compute an answer.
- We can ask things like who "bats – left" and "throws – right".

2. Inheritable Knowledge

- Here the knowledge elements inherit attributes from their parents.
- The knowledge is embodied in the design hierarchies found in the functional, physical and process domains.
- Within the hierarchy, elements inherit attributes from their parents, but in many cases not all attributes of the parent elements be prescribed to the child elements.
- The inheritance is a powerful form of inference, but not adequate.
- The basic KR (Knowledge Representation) needs to be augmented with inference mechanism.
- Property inheritance: The objects or elements of specific classes inherit attributes and values from more general classes.
- The classes are organized in a generalized hierarchy.

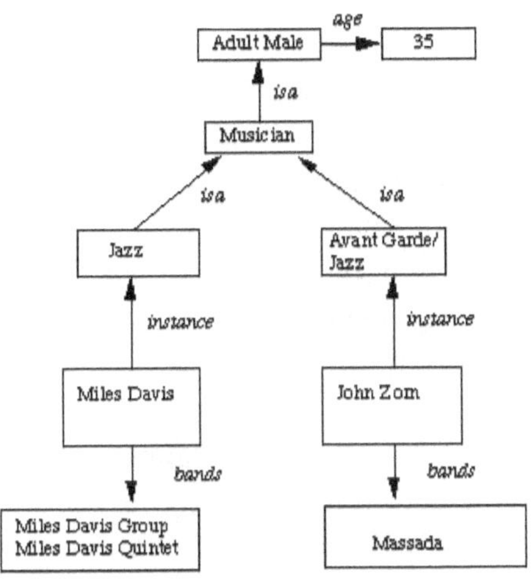

- Boxed nodes -- objects and values of attributes of objects.
- Arrows -- point from object to its value.
- This structure is known as a slot and filler structure, semantic network or a collection of frames.

○ The steps to retrieve a value for an attribute of an instance object:

ii. Find the object in the knowledge base
iii. If there is a value for the attribute report it
iv. Otherwise look for a value of an instance, if none fail
v. Otherwise go to that node and find a value for the attribute and then report it

vi. Otherwise search through using isa until a value is found for the attribute.

2. Inferential Knowledge

  - This knowledge generates new information from the given information.
  - This new information does not require further data gathering form source, but does require analysis of the given information to generate new knowledge.
  - Example: given a set of relations and values, one may infer other values or relations. A predicate logic (a mathematical deduction) is used to infer from a set of attributes. Inference through predicate logic uses a set of logical operations to relate individual data.
  - Represent knowledge as formal logic:

All dogs have tails $\forall$x: *dog(x)* $\rightarrow$ *hastail(x)*

  - Advantages:

    - A set of strict rules.
    - Can be used to derive more facts.
    - Truths of new statements can be verified.
    - Guaranteed correctness.

  - Many inference procedures available to implement standard rules of logic popular in AI

systems. e.g Automated theorem proving.

3. Procedural Knowledge

- A representation in which the control information, to use the knowledge, is embedded in the knowledge itself. For example, computer programs, directions, and recipes; these indicate specific use or implementation;
- Knowledge is encoded in some procedures, small programs that know how to do specific things, how to proceed.
- Advantages:

  - Heuristic or domain specific knowledge can be represented.
  - Extended logical inferences, such as default reasoning facilitated.
  - Side effects of actions may be modeled. Some rules may become false in time. Keeping track of this in large systems may be tricky.

- Disadvantages:

  - Completeness -- not all cases may be represented.
  - Consistency -- not all deductions may be correct. e.g If we know that Fred is a bird we might deduce that Fred can fly. Later we might discover that Fred is an emu.
  - Modularity is sacrificed. Changes in knowledge base might have far-reaching effects.
  - Cumbersome control information.

Issues in Knowledge Representation

- The fundamental goal of Knowledge Representation is to facilitate inference (conclusions) from knowledge.
- The issues that arise while using KR techniques are many. Some of these are explained below.

1. Important Attributes :

   - Any attribute of objects so basic that they occur in almost every problem domain?
   - There are two attributes "instance" and "isa", that are of general significance. These attributes are important because they support property inheritance.

2. Relationship among attributes:

   - Any important relationship that exists among object attributes?
   - The attributes we use to describe objects are themselves entities that we represent.
   - The relationship between the attributes of an object, independent of specific knowledge they encode, may hold properties like:

i. Inverses - This is about consistency check, while a value is added to one attribute. The entities are related to each other in many different ways.

ii. Existence in an *isa* hierarchy - This is about generalization-specialization, like, classes of objects and specialized subsets of those classes, there are attributes and specialization of attributes. For example, the attribute height is a specialization of general attribute physical-size which is, in turn, a specialization of physical-attribute. These generalization-specialization relationships are

important for attributes because they support inheritance.

iii. Techniques for reasoning about values - This is about reasoning values of attributes not given explicitly. Several kinds of information are used in reasoning, like,

height : must be in a unit of length,
Age: of person cannot be greater than the age of person's parents.
The values are often specified when a knowledge base is created.

iv. Single valued attributes - This is about a specific attribute that is guaranteed to take a unique value. For example, a baseball player can at time have only a single height and be a member of only one team. KR systems take different approaches to provide support for single valued attributes.

3. Choosing Granularity :

   ○ At what level of detail should the knowledge be represented?
   ○ Regardless of the KR formalism, it is necessary to know :

     ▪ At what level should the knowledge be represented and what are the primitives?"

- Should there be a small number or should there be a large number of low-level primitives or High-level facts.
- High-level facts may not be adequate for inference while Low-level primitives may require a lot of storage.

- Example of Granularity :

  - Suppose we are interested in following facts: John spotted Sue.

This could be represented as
Spotted (agent(John), object (Sue))
– Such a representation would make it easy to answer questions such are :

  - Who spotted Sue? Suppose we want to know :
  - Did John see Sue?

– Given only one fact, we cannot discover that answer.
– We can add other facts, such as
Spotted (x , y) $\rightarrow$ saw (x , y)
– We can now infer the answer to the question.

4. Set of objects :

  - How should sets of objects be represented?
  - There are certain properties of objects that are true as member of a set but not as individual;

- Example : Consider the assertion made in the sentences : "there are more sheep than people in Australia", and "English speakers can be found all over the world."

- To describe these facts, the only way is to attach assertion to the sets representing people, sheep, and English.
- The reason to represent sets of objects is: If a property is true for all or most elements of a set, then it is more efficient to associate it once with the set rather than to associate it explicitly with every elements of the set .
- This is done,

    - in logical representation through the use of universal quantifier, and
    - in hierarchical structure where node represent sets and inheritance propagate set level assertion down to individual.

5. Finding Right structure :

   ○ Given a large amount of knowledge stored in a database, how can relevant parts are accessed when they are needed?
   ○ This is about access to right structure for describing a particular situation.
   ○ This requires, selecting an initial structure and then revising the choice.
   ○ While doing so, it is necessary to solve following problems :

- how to perform an initial selection of the most appropriate structure.
- how to fill in appropriate details from the current situations.
- how to find a better structure if the one chosen initially turns out not to be appropriate.
- what to do if none of the available structures is appropriate.
- when to create and remember a new structure.

○ There is no good, general purpose method for solving all these problems. Some knowledge representation techniques solve some of these issues.

CHAPTER FOUR

Using Predicate Logic

Logic

- The logical formalism of a language is useful because it immediately suggests a powerful way of deriving new knowledge from old using mathematical deduction.
- In this formalism, we can conclude that a new statement is true by proving that it follows from the statements that are already known.

Proposition

- A proposition is a statement, or a simple declarative sentence.
- For example, "the book is expensive" is a proposition.
- A proposition can be either true or false.

Propositional logic

- Logical constants: true, false
- Propositional symbols: P, Q, S,... (atomic sentences)

Propositions are combined by connectives:

$\wedge$	and	[conjunction]
$\vee$	or	[disjunction]
$\Rightarrow$	implies	[implication]
$\neg$	not	[negation]
$\forall$	For all	
$\exists$	There exists	

- Propositional logic is a simple language useful for showing key ideas and definitions.
- User defines a set of propositional symbols, like P and Q.
- User defines the semantics of each propositional symbol:

P means "It is hot"
Q means "It is humid" R means "It is raining"

- A sentence (well-formed formula) is defined as follows:

- ◦ A symbol is a sentence.
- ◦ If S is a sentence, then Ø S is a sentence.
- ◦ If S is a sentence, then (S) is a sentence.
- ◦ If S and T are sentences, then (S Ú T), (S Ù T), (S ® T), and (S ↔ T) are sentences
- ◦ A sentence results from a finite number of applications of the above rules.

- ***Real world facts can be represented by well-formed formulas (wffs) in propositional logic.***

Representation of Simple Facts in Logic

- Propositional logic is useful because it is simple to deal with and a decision procedure for it exists.
- In order to draw conclusions, facts are represented in a more convenient way as,

1. Marcus is a man. man(Marcus)
2. Plato is a man. man(Plato)
3. All men are mortal. mortal(men)

- But propositional logic fails to capture the relationship between any individual being a man and that individual being a mortal.

  - How can these sentences be represented so that we can infer the third sentence from the first two?
  - Propositional logic commits only to the existence of facts that may or may not be the case in the world

being represented.
- It has a simple syntax and simple semantics. It suffices to illustrate the process of inference.
- Propositional logic quickly becomes impractical, even for very small worlds.

Predicate logic

- First-order Predicate logic (FOPL) models the world in terms of

  ○ Objects, which are things with individual identities
  ○ Properties of objects that distinguish them from other objects
  ○ Relations that hold among sets of objects
  ○ Functions, which are a subset of relations where there is only one "value" for any given "input"

- First-order Predicate logic (FOPL) provides

  ○ Constants: a, b, dog33. Name a specific object.
  ○ Variables: X, Y. Refer to an object without naming it.
  ○ Functions: Mapping from objects to objects.
  ○ Terms: Refer to objects
  ○ Atomic Sentences: in(dad-of(X), food6) Can be true or false, Correspond to propositional symbols P, Q.

  ○ A well-formed formula (*wff*) is a sentence containing no "free" variables. That is, all variables are "bound" by universal or existential quantifiers.

  ("x)P(x, y) has x bound as a universally quantified variable, but y is free.

Quantifiers

- Universal quantification

("x)P(x) means that P holds for all values of x in the domain associated with that
variable
E.g., ("x) dolphin(x) ® mammal(x)

- Existential quantification

($ x)P(x) means that P holds for some value of x in the domain associated with that variable
E.g., ($ x) mammal(x) Ù lays-eggs(x)

- Consider the following example that shows the use of predicate logic as a way of representing knowledge.

1. Marcus was a man.
2. Marcus was a Pompeian.
3. All Pompeians were Romans.
4. Caesar was a ruler.
5. All Pompeians were either loyal to Caesar or hated him.
6. Everyone is loyal to someone.
7. People only try to assassinate rulers they are not loyal to.
8. Marcus tried to assassinate Caesar.

- The facts described by these sentences can be represented as a set of well-formed formulas (*wffs*) as follows:

1. Marcus was a man.

man(Marcus)

1. Marcus was a Pompeian. Pompeian(Marcus)
2. All Pompeians were Romans.

    "x: Pompeian(x) ® Roman(x)

4. Caesar was a ruler.

    ruler(Caesar)

5. All Pompeians were either loyal to Caesar or hated him.

    inclusive-or
    "x: Roman(x) ® loyalto(x, Caesar) Ú hate(x, Caesar)
    exclusive-or
           "x: Roman(x) ® (loyalto(x, Caesar) Ù Øhate(x,
                        Caesar)) Ú
             (Øloyalto(x, Caesar) Ù hate(x, Caesar))

6. Every-one is loyal to someone.

    "x: $y: loyalto(x, y)

7. People only try to assassinate rulers they are not loyal
    to.

    "x: "y: person(x) Ù ruler(y) Ù tryassassinate(x, y)
    ® Øloyalto(x, y)

8. Marcus tried to assassinate Caesar.
    tryassassinate(Marcus, Caesar)

- Now suppose if we want to use these statements to answer the question

Was Marcus loyal to Caesar?

- Now let's try to produce a formal proof, reasoning backward from the desired goal:

¬ Ioyalto(Marcus, Caesar)

- In order to prove the goal, we need to use the rules of inference to transform it into another goal (or possibly a set of goals) that can in turn be transformed, and so on, until there are no unsatisfied goals remaining.

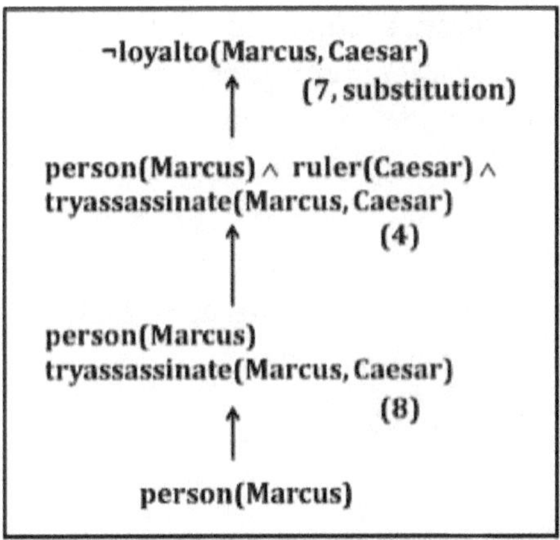

Figure 4.1 An attempt to prove ¬loyalto(Marcus, Caesar).

- The problem is that, although we know that Marcus was a man, we do not have any way to conclude from that that Marcus was a person. We need to add the representation of another fact to our system, namely:

$$\forall : man(x) \rightarrow person(x)$$

- Now we can satisfy the last goal and produce a proof that Marcus was not loyal to Caesar.
- From this simple example, we see that three important issues must be addressed in the process of converting English sentences into logical statements and then using those statements to deduce new ones:

1. Many English sentences are ambiguous (for example, 5, 6, and 7 above). Choosing the correct interpretation may be difficult.
2. There is often a choice of how to represent the knowledge. Simple representations are desirable, but they may exclude certain kinds of reasoning.
3. Even in very simple situations, a set of sentences is unlikely to contain all the information necessary to reason about the topic at hand. In order to be able to use a set of statements effectively, it is usually necessary to have access to another set of statements that represent facts that people consider too obvious to mention.

Representing INSTANCE and *ISA* Relationships

- Specific attributes **instance** and **isa** play important role particularly in a useful form of reasoning called property inheritance.
- *The predicates instance and isa explicitly captured the relationships they are used to express, namely class membership and class inclusion.*
- Fig. 4.2 shows the first five sentences of the last section represented in logic in three different ways.
- The first part of the figure contains the representations we have already discussed. In these representations, class membership is represented with unary predicates (such as Roman), each of which corresponds to a class.
- Asserting that $P(x)$ is true is equivalent to asserting that x is an instance (or element) of P.

The second part of the figure contains representations that use the **instance** predicate explicitly.

<table>
<tr><td>1.</td><td>Man(Marcus).</td></tr>
<tr><td>2.</td><td>Pompeian(Marcus).</td></tr>
<tr><td>3.</td><td>$\forall x$: Pompeian(x) $\rightarrow$ Roman(x).</td></tr>
<tr><td>4.</td><td>ruler(Caesar).</td></tr>
<tr><td>5.</td><td>$\forall x$: Roman(x) $\rightarrow$ loyalto(x, Caesar) $\vee$ hate(x, Caesar).</td></tr>
<tr><td>1.</td><td>instance(Marcus, man).</td></tr>
<tr><td>2.</td><td>instance(Marcus, Pompeian).</td></tr>
<tr><td>3.</td><td>$\forall x$: instance(x, Pompeian) $\rightarrow$ instance(x, Roman).</td></tr>
<tr><td>4.</td><td>instance(Caesar, ruler).</td></tr>
<tr><td>5.</td><td>$\forall x$: instance(x, Roman). $\rightarrow$ loyalto(x, Caesar) $\vee$ hate(x, Caesar).</td></tr>
<tr><td>1.</td><td>instance(Marcus, man).</td></tr>
<tr><td>2.</td><td>instance(Marcus, Pompeian).</td></tr>
<tr><td>3.</td><td>isa(Pompeian, Roman)</td></tr>
<tr><td>4.</td><td>instance(Caesar, ruler).</td></tr>
<tr><td>5.</td><td>$\forall x$: instance(x, Roman). $\rightarrow$ loyalto(x, Caesar) $\vee$ hate(x, Caesar).</td></tr>
<tr><td>6.</td><td>$\forall x$: $\forall y$: $\forall z$: instance(x, y) $\wedge$ isa(y, z) $\rightarrow$ instance(x, z).</td></tr>
</table>

Figure 4.2 Three ways of representing class membership

- The predicate *instance* is a binary one, whose first argument is an object and whose second argument is a class to which the object belongs.

- But these representations do not use an explicit *isa* predicate.

- Instead, subclass relationships, such as that between Pompeians and Romans, are described as shown in sentence 3.

- The implication rule states that if an object is an instance of the subclass Pompeian then it is an instance of the superclass Roman.

- Note that this rule is equivalent to the standard set-theoretic definition of the subclass- superclass

78

relationship.

- The third part contains representations that use both the *instance* and *isa* predicates explicitly.
- The use of the *isa* predicate simplifies the representation of sentence 3, but it requires that one additional axiom (shown here as number 6) be provided.

Computable Functions and Predicates

- To express simple facts, such as the following greater-than and less-than relationships: gt(1,O) It(0,1)

gt(2,1) It(1,2)
gt(3,2) It(2,3)

- It is often also useful to have computable functions as well as computable predicates. Thus we might want to be able to evaluate the truth of

gt(2 + 3,1)

- To do so requires that we first compute the value of the plus function given the arguments 2 and 3, and then send the arguments 5 and 1 to gt.
- Consider the following set of facts, again involving Marcus:

1. Marcus was a man.

man(Marcus)

1. Marcus was a Pompeian. Pompeian(Marcus)
2. Marcus was born in 40 A.D. born(Marcus, 40)
3. All men are mortal.

$\forall x: man(x) \rightarrow mortal(x)$

5. All Pompeians died when the volcano erupted in 79 A.D. erupted(volcano, 79) ? $\forall x$: [Pompeian(x) $\rightarrow$ died(x, 79)]
6. No mortal lives longer than 150 years.

$\forall x: \forall t1: At2: mortal(x) ? born(x, t1) ? gt(t2 - t1,150) \rightarrow died(x, t2)$

7. It is now 1991.

$now = 1991$

- Above example shows how these ideas of computable functions and predicates can be useful.

- It also makes use of the notion of equality and allows equal objects to be substituted for each other whenever it appears helpful to do so during a proof.
- Now suppose we want to answer the question "Is Marcus alive?"
- The statements suggested here, there may be two ways of deducing an answer.
- Either we can show that Marcus is dead because he was killed by the volcano or we can show that he

must be dead because he would otherwise be more than 150 years old, which we know is not possible.

- As soon as we attempt to follow either of those paths rigorously, however, we discover, just as we did in the last example, that we need some additional knowledge. For example, our statements talk about dying, but they say nothing that relates to being alive, which is what the question is asking.
- So we add the following facts:

8. Alive means not dead.

$\forall x: \forall t: [\text{alive}(x, t) \rightarrow \neg \text{dead}(x, t)] ? [\neg \text{dead}(x, t) \rightarrow \text{alive}(x, t)]$

9. If someone dies, then he is dead at all later times.

$\forall x: \forall t1: \text{A}t2: died(x, t1) ? gt(t2, t1) \rightarrow dead(x, t2)$

- Now let's attempt to answer the question "Is Marcus alive?" by proving:

$\neg$ *alive(Marcus, now)*

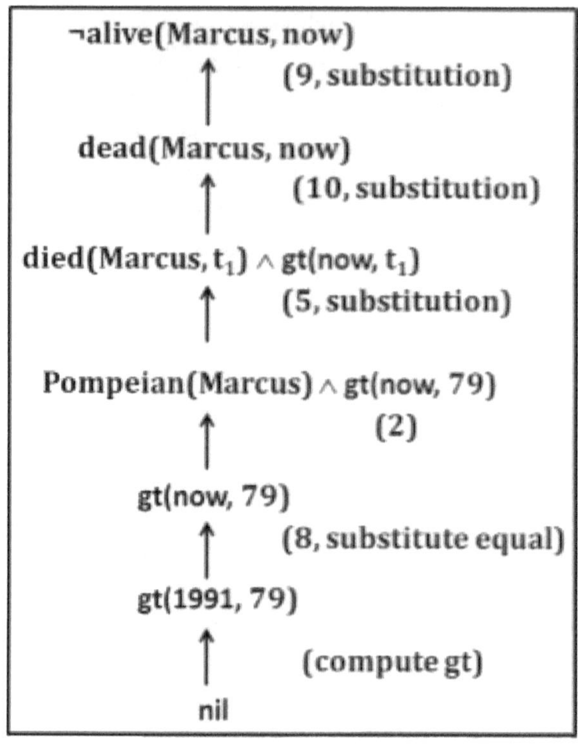

Resolution

- Resolution is a procedure, which gains its efficiency from the fact that it operates on statements that have been converted to a very convenient standard form.

- Resolution produces proofs by refutation.

- *In other words, to prove a statement (i.e., to show that it is valid), resolution attempts to show that the negation of the statement produces a contradiction with the known statements (i.e., that it is unsatisfiable).*
- The resolution procedure is a simple iterative process: at each step, two clauses, called the parent clauses, are compared (resolved), resulting into a new clause that has been inferred from them. The new clause represents ways that the two parent clauses interact with each other. Suppose that there are two clauses in the system:

winter V summer
¬ winter V cold

- Now we observe that precisely one of winter and ¬ winter will be true at any point.
- If winter is true, then cold must be true to guarantee the truth of the second clause. If ¬ winter is true, then summer must be true to guarantee the truth of the first clause.
- Thus we see that from these two clauses we can deduce

summer V cold

- This is the deduction that the resolution procedure will make.
- Resolution operates by taking two clauses that each contains the same literal, in this example, **winter**.
- The literal must occur in positive form in one clause and in negative form in the other. The resolvent is obtained by combining all of the literals of the two parent clauses except the ones that cancel.

- If the clause that is produced is the empty clause, then a contradiction has been found.

  For example, the two clauses winter
  ¬ winter
  will produce the empty clause.
  Conversion to Clause form

- To apply resolution, we need to reduce a set of *wff's* to a set of clauses, where a clause is defined to be a *wff* in conjunctive normal form but with no instances of the connector A.
- We can do this by first converting each wff into conjunctive normal form and then breaking apart each such expression into clauses, one for each conjunct.
- All the conjuncts will be considered to be conjoined together as the proof procedure operates. To convert a *wff* into clause form, perform the following sequence of steps.

Algorithm: Convert to Clause Form

1. Eliminate $\rightarrow$, using the fact that a $\rightarrow$ b is equivalent to ¬ a V b. Performing this transformation on the wff given above becomes

   ∀x: ¬ [Roman(x) ? know(x, Marcus)] V
   [hate(x, Caesar) V (∀y : ¬(∃z : hate(y, z)) V thinkcrazy(x, y))]

1. Reduce the scope of each ¬ to a single term, using the fact that ¬ (¬ p) = p, Performing this transformation on

the wff from step 1 becomes

∀x: [¬ Roman(x) V ¬ know(x, Marcus)] V
**[hate(x, Caesar) V (∀y: ∀z: ¬ hate(y, z) V
thinkcrazy(x, y))]**

3. Standardize variables so that each quantifier binds a unique variable. Since variables are just dummy names, this process cannot affect the truth value of the wff.

For example, the formula ∀x: P(x) V ∀x: Q(x) would be converted to ∀x: P(x) V ∀y: Q(y)

4. Move all quantifiers to the left of the formula without changing their relative order. This is possible since there is no conflict among variable names. Performing this operation on the formula of step 2, we get

∀x: ∀y: Az: [¬ Roman(x) V ¬ know(x, Marcus)] V [hate(x, Caesar) V (¬ hale(y, z) V thinkcrazy(x, y))]

5. Eliminate existential quantifiers. So, for example, the formula

∃y : President(y)
          can be transformed into the formula
President(S1)
          For example, in the formula
∀x: ∃y: father-of(y, x)
          would be transformed into
∀x: father-of(S2(x), x)

These generated functions are called Skolem functions. Sometimes ones with no arguments are called Skolem constants.

6. Drop the prefix. At this point, all remaining variables are universally quantified, so the prefix can just be dropped and any proof procedure we use can simply assume that any variable it sees is universally quantified. Now the formula produced in step 4 appears as

$[\neg$ Roman(x) V $\neg$ know$(x,$ Marcus$)]$ V
[hate(x, Caesar) V ($\neg$ hate(y, z) V thinkcrazy(x, y))]

7. Convert the matrix into a conjunction of disjuncts. In the case or our example, since there are no and's, it is only necessary to exploit the associative property of or [i.e., (a ? b) V c = (a V c) ? (b ? c)] and simply remove the parentheses, giving

$\neg$ Roman(x) V $\neg$ know$(x,$ Marcus$)$ V
hate(x, Caesar) V $\neg$ hate(y, z) V thinkcrazy(x, y)

8. Create a separate clause corresponding to each conjunct. In order for a wff to be true, all the clauses that are generated from it must be true.
9. Standardize apart the variables in the set of clauses generated in step 8. By this we mean rename the variables so that no two clauses make reference to the same variable. In making this transformation, we rely on the fact that

($\forall$x: P(x) ? Q(x)) = $\forall$x: P(x) ? $\forall$x: Q(x)

Thus since each clause is a separate conjunct and since all the variables are universally

quantified, there need be no relationship between the variables of two clauses, even if they were generated from the same wff.

Algorithm: Propositional Resolution

1. Convert all the propositions of F to clause form.
2. Negate P and convert the result to clause form. Add it to the set of clauses obtained in step 1.
3. Repeat until either a contradiction is found or no progress can be made:

   a. Select two clauses. Call these the parent clauses.
   b. Resolve them together. The resulting clause, called the resolvent, will be the disjunction of all of the literals of both of the parent clauses with the following exception: If there are any pairs of literals L and $\neg L$ such that one of the parent clauses contains L and the other contains $\neg L$, then select one such pair and eliminate both L and $\neg L$ from the resolvent.
   c. If the resolvent is the empty clause, then a contradiction has been found. If it is not, then add it to the set of clauses available to the procedure.

The Unification Algorithm

- In propositional logic, it is easy to determine that two literals cannot both be true at the same time.
- Simply look for L and ¬L in predicate logic, this matching process is more complicated since the arguments of the predicates must be considered.

- For example, man(John) and ¬man(John) is a contradiction, while man(John) and

  ¬man(Spot) is not.

- Thus, in order to determine contradictions, we need a matching procedure that compares two literals and discovers whether there exists a set of substitutions that makes them identical.
- There is a straightforward recursive procedure, called the unification algorithm, that does it.

Algorithm: Unify(L1, L2)

1. If L1 or L2 are both variables or constants, then:

   a. If L1 and L2 are identical, then return NIL.
   b. Else if L1 is a variable, then if L1 occurs in L2 then return {FAIL}, else return (L2/L1).
   c. Else if L2 is a variable, then if L2 occurs in L1 then return {FAIL}, else return (L1/L2).
   d. Else return {FAIL}.

2. If the initial predicate symbols in L1 and L2 are not identical, then return {FAIL}.
3. If LI and L2 have a different number of arguments, then return {FAIL}.
4. Set SUBST to NIL. (At the end of this procedure, SUBST will contain all the substitutions used to unify L1 and L2.)
5. For i ← 1 to number of arguments in L1 :

a. Call Unify with the ith argument of L1 and the ith argument of L2, putting result in S.
b. If S contains FAIL then return {FAIL}.
c. If S is not equal to NIL then:

    i. Apply S to the remainder of both L1 and L2.
    ii. SUBST: = APPEND(S, SUBST).

6. Return SUBST.

Resolution in Predicate Logic

- We can now state the resolution algorithm for predicate logic as follows, assuming a set of given statements F and a statement to be proved P:

Algorithm: Resolution

1. Convert all the statements of F to clause form.
2. Negate P and convert the result to clause form. Add it to the set of clauses obtained in 1.
3. Repeat until a contradiction is found, no progress can be made, or a predetermined amount of effort has been expended.

    a. Select two clauses. Call these the parent clauses.
    b. Resolve them together. The resolvent will be the disjunction of all the literals of both parent clauses with appropriate substitutions performed and with the following exception: If there is one pair of literals T1 and ¬T2 such that one of the parent clauses contains T2 and the other contains T1 and if T1 and T2 are unifiable, then neither T1 nor T2 should

appear in the resolvent. We call T1 and T2 Complementary literals. Use the substitution produced by the unification to create the resolvent. If there is more than one pair of complementary literals, only one pair should be omitted from the resolvent.

c. If the resolvent is an empty clause, then a contradiction has been found. If it is not, then add it to the set of clauses available to the procedure.

Example: Consider the following facts. Translate given sentences into formulas in predicate logic. Prove by resolution the given fact.

1. Marcus was a man.
2. Marcus was a Pompeian.
3. All pompeians were Romans.
4. Caesar was a ruler.
5. All Romans were either loyal to Caesar or hated him.
6. Everyone is loyal to someone.
7. People only try to assassinate rulers they are not loyal to.
8. Marcus tried to assassinate Caesar.

Prove: hate (Marcus, Caesar)
<u>Solution:</u>
Predicate logic statements.

1. Marcus was a man.

man(Marcus)

2. Marcus was a Pompeian. Pompeian(Marcus)

3. All Pompeians were Romans.

"x: Pompeian(x) ® Roman(x)

4. Caesar was a ruler.

ruler(Caesar)

5. All Pompeians were either loyal to Caesar or hated him.

"x: Roman(x) ® loyalto(x, Caesar) Ú hate(x, Caesar)

6. Every-one is loyal to someone.

"x: $y: loyalto(x, y)

7. People only try to assassinate rulers they are not loyal to.

"x: "y: person(x) Ù ruler(y) Ù tryassassinate(x, y)
® Øloyalto(x, y)

8. Marcus tried to assassinate Caesar.
tryassassinate(Marcus, Caesar)

Axioms in clause form –

1. man(Marcus)
2. Pompeian(Marcus)
3. ¬Pompeian(x1) \/ Roman(x1)
4. ruler(Caesar)
5. ¬Roman(x2) \/ loyalto(x2, Caesar) \/ hate(x2, Caesar)

6. loyalto(x3,fl(x3))
7. ¬man(x4) $\bigvee$ ¬ruler(y1) $\bigvee$ ¬tryassassinate(x4,y1) $\bigvee$ loyalto(x4,y1)
8. trayassassinate(Marcus,Caesar)

CHAPTER FIVE

Representing Knowledge Using Rules

Introduction

- We have discussed various search techniques in previous units. Now we would consider a set of rules that represents,

i. Knowledge about relationships in the world and
ii. Knowledge about how to solve problem using the content of the rules.

Procedural versus Declarative Knowledge

Procedural Knowledge

- A representation in which the control information that is necessary to use the knowledge is embedded in the knowledge itself for e.g. computer programs, directions, and recipes; these indicate specific use or implementation;
- The real difference between declarative and procedural views of knowledge lies in where control information reside.
- For example, consider the following

Man (Marcus) Man (Caesar) Person (Cleopatra)
∀ x: Man(x) à Person(x)
Now, try to answer the question. ?Person(y)
The knowledge base justifies any of the following answers.
Y=Marcus Y=Caesar Y=Cleopatra

- We get more than one value that satisfies the predicate.
- If only one value is needed, then the answer to the question will depend on the order in which the assertions are examined during the search for a response.
- If the assertions are declarative then they do not themselves say anything about how they will be examined. In case of procedural representation, they say how they will be examined.

Declarative Knowledge

- A statement in which knowledge is specified, but the use to which that knowledge is to be put is not given.

- For example, laws, people's name; these are the facts which can stand alone, not dependent on other knowledge;
- So to use declarative representation, we must have a program that explains what is to be done to the knowledge and how.
- For example, a set of logical assertions can be combined with a resolution theorem prover to give a complete program for solving problems but in some cases the logical assertions can be viewed as a program rather than data to a program.
- Hence the implication statements define the legitimate reasoning paths and automatic

assertions provide the starting points of those paths.

- These paths define the execution paths which is similar to the 'if then else "in traditional programming.
- So logical assertions can be viewed as a procedural representation of knowledge.

Differences Between Declarative knowledge and procedural knowledge

Procedural knowledge	Declarative knowledge
High efficiency	Higher level of abstraction
Low modifiability	Good modifiability and good readability
Low perceptive adequacy (better for knowledge engineers)	Suitable for independent facts
Produces creative, reflective thought and promoters critical thinking and independent decision making	Good cognitive matching (better for domain experts and end-users) and low computational efficiency.

Logic Programming

- Logic programming is a programming paradigm in which logical assertions are viewed as programs.
- These are several logic programming systems, PROLOG is one of them.
- *A PROLOG program consists of several logical assertions where each is a horn clause i.e. a clause with at most one positive literal.*

Ex : P, P V Q, P à Q

- The facts are represented on Horn Clause for two reasons.

    i. Because of a uniform representation, a simple and efficient interpreter can be written.
    ii. The logic of Horn Clause is decidable.

- The first two differences are from the fact that PROLOG programs are actually sets of Horn clause that have been transformed as follows:-

1. If the Horn Clause contains no negative literal then leave it as it is.
2. Otherwise rewrite the Horn clauses as an implication, combining all of the negative literals in to the antecedent of the implications and the single positive literal into the consequent.

- This procedure causes a clause which originally consisted of a disjunction of literals (one of them was positive) to be transformed into a single implication whose antecedent is a conjunction universally quantified.
- But when we apply this transformation, any variables that occurred in negative literals and so now occur in the antecedent become existentially quantified, while the variables in the consequent are still universally quantified.

  - For example the PROLOG clause P(x): - Q(x, y) is equal to logical expression "x: $y: Q (x, y) à

- P(x).

  - The difference between the logic and PROLOG representation is that the PROLOG interpretation has a fixed control strategy and so the assertions in the PROLOG program define a particular search path to answer to any question.
  - But, the logical assertions define only the set of answers but not about how to choose among those answers if there is more than one.
  - Consider the following example:

- Logical representation
- "$x : pet(x) \land small\ (x)$ à $apartmentpet(x)$
  " $x : cat(x) \lor dog(x)$ à $pet(x)$
  "$x : poodle\ (x)$ à $dog\ (x) \land small\ (x)$ poodle (fluffy)
- Prolog representation

- *apartmentpet (x) : -- pet(x), small (x) pet (x): -- cat (x)*

  pet (x) :-- dog(x)
  dog(x) :-- poodle (x)
  small (x) :-- poodle(x) poodle (fluffy)

Forward versus Backward Reasoning

- A search procedure must find a path between initial and goal states.
- There are two directions in which a search process could proceed.
- The two types of search are:

- Forward search which starts from the start state
- Backward search that starts from the goal state

  - The production system views the forward and backward as symmetric processes.
  - Consider a game of playing 8 puzzles. The rules defined are

- *Square 1 empty and square 2 contains tile n. à*

  - *Square 2 empty and square 1 contains the tile n.*

- *Square 1 empty Square 4 contains tile n. à*

  - *Square 4 empty and Square 1 contains tile n.*

  - We can solve the problem in 2 ways:

- Reason forward from the initial state

  - Step 1. Begin building a tree of move sequences by starting with the initial configuration at the root of the tree.
  - Step 2. Generate the next level of tree by finding all rules *whose left hand side matches* against the root node. The right hand side is used to create new

-     configurations.

  - Step 3. Generate the next level by considering the nodes in the previous level and applying it to all rules whose left hand side match.

- Reasoning backward from the goal states:

  - Step 1. Begin building a tree of move sequences by starting with the goal node configuration at the root of the tree.
  - Step 2. Generate the next level of tree by finding all rules *whose right hand side matches* against the root node. The left hand side is used to create new configurations.
  - Step 3. Generate the next level by considering the nodes in the previous level and applying it to all rules whose right hand side match.

  - The same rules can be used in both cases.
  - In forward reasoning the left hand sides of the rules are matched against the current state and right sides are used to generate the new state.

- In backward reasoning the right hand sides of the rules are matched against the current state and left sides are used to generate the new state.
- There are four factors influencing the type of reasoning. They are,

- Are there more possible start or goal state? We move from smaller set of sets to the longer.
- In what direction is the branching factor greater? We proceed in the direction with the lower branching factor.
- Will the program be asked to justify its reasoning process to a user? If, so then it is selected since it is very close to the way in which the user thinks.
- What kind of event is going to trigger a problem-solving episode? If it is the arrival of a new factor, forward reasoning makes sense. If it is a query to which a response is desired, backward reasoning is more natural.

- Example 1: It is easier to drive from an unfamiliar place from home, rather than from home to an unfamiliar place. If you consider a home as starting place an unfamiliar place as a goal then we have to back track from unfamiliar place to home.
- Example 2: Consider a problem of symbolic integration. The problem space is a set of formulas, which contains integral expressions. Here START is equal to the given formula with some integrals. GOAL is equivalent to the expression of the formula without any integral. Here we start from the formula with some

integrals and proceed to an integral free expression rather than starting from an integral free expression.

- Example 3: The third factor is nothing but deciding whether the reasoning process can justify its reasoning. If it justifies then it can be applied. For example, doctors are usually unwilling to accept any advice from diagnostics process because it cannot explain its reasoning.
- Example 4: Prolog is an example of backward chaining rule system. In Prolog rules are restricted to Horn clauses. This allows for rapid indexing because all the rules for deducing a given fact share the same rule head. Rules are matched with unification procedure. Unification tries to find a set of bindings for variables to equate a sub-goal with the head of some rule. Rules in the Prolog program are matched in the order in which they appear.

- Combining Forward and Backward Reasoning

  - Instead of searching either forward or backward, you can search both simultaneously.
  - That is, start forward from a stating state and backward from a goal state simultaneously until the paths meet.
  - This strategy is called Bi-directional search. The following figure shows the reason for Bi-directional search to be ineffective.

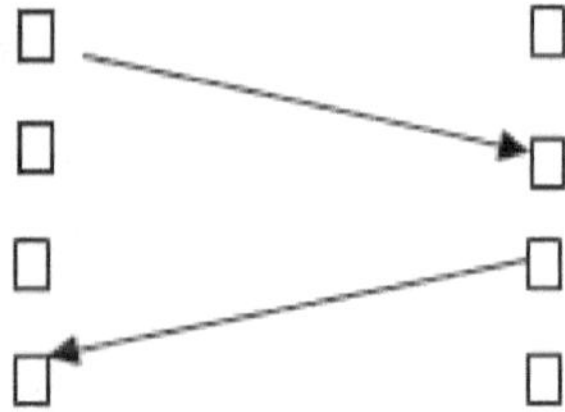

- The two searches may pass each other resulting in more work.
- Based on the form of the rules one can decide whether the same rules can be applied for both forward and backward reasoning.
- If left hand side and right of the rule contain pure assertions then the rule can be reversed. And so the same rule can be applied for both types of reasoning.
- If the right side of the rule contains an arbitrary procedure then the rule cannot be reversed.
- In this case while writing the rule the commitment to direction of reasoning must be made.

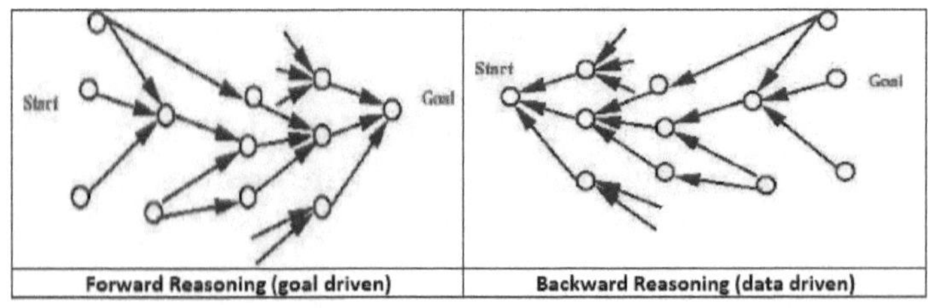

Enter Caption

103

CHAPTER SIX

SYMBOLIC REASONING UNDER UNCERTAINTY

What is Reasoning

- Reasoning is the act of deriving a conclusion from certain properties using a given methodology.
- Reasoning is a process of thinking; reasoning is logically arguing; reasoning is drawing inference.
- *When a system is required to do something, that it has not been explicitly told how to do, it must reason. It must figure out what it needs to know from what it already knows.*
- Many types of Reasoning have been identified and recognized, but many questions regarding their logical and computational properties still remain

controversial.

- The popular methods of Reasoning include abduction, induction, model-based, explanation and confirmation. All of them are intimately related to problems of belief revision and theory development, knowledge absorption, discovery and learning.

Logical Reasoning

- Logic is a language for reasoning. It is a collection of rules called Logic arguments, we use when doing logical reasoning.
- Logic reasoning is the process of drawing conclusions from premises using rules of inference.
- The study of logic is divided into formal and informal logic. The formal logic is sometimes called symbolic logic.
- Symbolic logic is the study of symbolic abstractions (construct) that capture the formal features of logical inference by a formal system.
- Formal system consists of two components, a formal language plus a set of inference rules.
- The formal system has axioms. Axiom is a sentence that is always true within the system.
- Sentences are derived using the system's axioms and rules of derivation are called theorems.
- The Logical Reasoning is of our concern in AI.

Approaches to Reasoning

- There are three different approaches to reasoning under uncertainties.

1. Symbolic reasoning
2. Statistical reasoning
3. Fuzzy logic reasoning

Symbolic Reasoning

- The basis for intelligent mathematical software is the integration of the "power of symbolic mathematical tools" with the suitable "proof technology".
- Mathematical reasoning enjoys a property called monotonicity, that says, "If a conclusion follows from given premises A, B, C, ... then it also follows from any larger set of premises, as long as the original premises A, B, C, ... are included."
- Human reasoning is not monotonic.
- People arrive to conclusions only tentatively; based on partial or incomplete information,

reserve the right to retract those conclusions while they learn new facts. Such reasoning is non-monotonic, precisely because the set of accepted conclusions have become smaller when the set of premises is expanded.

Formal Logic

- The Formal logic is the study of inference with purely formal content, i.e. where content is made explicit.
- Examples - Propositional logic and Predicate logic.
- Here the logical arguments are a set of rules for manipulating symbols. The rules are of two types,

1. Syntax rules: say how to build meaningful expressions.

2. Inference rules: say how to obtain true formulas from other true formulas.

- Logic also needs semantics, which says how to assign meaning to expressions.

Uncertainty in Reasoning

- The world is an uncertain place; often the Knowledge is imperfect which causes uncertainty. Therefore reasoning must be able to operate under uncertainty.
- AI systems must have ability to reason under conditions of uncertainty.

Uncertainties	Desired action
Incompleteness of Knowledge	Compensate for lack of knowledge
Inconsistencies of Knowledge	Resolve ambiguities and contradictions
Changing Knowledge	Update the knowledge base over time

Monotonic Reasoning

- A reasoning process that moves in one direction only.
- The number of facts in the knowledge base is always increasing.
- The conclusions derived are valid deductions and they remain so.

A monotonic logic cannot handle,

a. Reasoning by default: because consequences may be derived only because of lack of evidence of the contrary.
b. Abductive reasoning: because consequences are only deduced as most likely explanations.
c. Belief revision: because new knowledge may contradict old beliefs.

Introduction to Non-monotonic Reasoning

- Non-monotonic reasoning (NMR) is based on supplementing absolute truth with beliefs.
- These tentative beliefs are generally based on default assumptions that are made in light of lack of evidence.
- A non-monotonic reasoning (NMR) system tracks a set of tentative beliefs and revises those beliefs when knowledge is observed or derived.
- The reason is, the human reasoning is non-monotonic in nature.
- This means, we reach to conclusions from certain premises that we would not reach if certain other sentences are included in our premises.

- Conventional reasoning systems such as first order predicate logic are designed to work with information that has three important properties.

1. It is complete with respect to the domain of interest.
2. It is consistent.
3. The only way it can change is that new facts can be added as they become available. If the new facts

are consistent with all other facts that have already been asserted, then nothing will be ever retracted from the set of facts that are known to be true. This property is called monotonicity.

- Non-monotonic reasoning systems are designed to be able to solve problems in which above three properties may be missing.
- In order to do this, following key issues must be addressed.

1. How can knowledge base be extended to allow inferences to be made on the basis of lack of knowledge as well as on the presence of it?
2. How can the knowledge base be updated properly when a new fact is added to the system or when an old one is removed?
3. How can knowledge be used to help resolve conflicts when there are several in consistent non-monotonic inferences that could be drawn?

Logics for Non-monotonic Reasoning

- A non-monotonic logic is a formal logic whose consequence relation is not monotonic.
- Logic is non-monotonic if the truth of a proposition may change when new information (axioms) is added.
- Allows a statement to be retracted.
- Used to formalize plausible (believable) reasoning.

Example 1 :
Birds typically fly. Tweety is a bird. Tweety (presumably) flies.

- Conclusion of non-monotonic argument may not be correct.

Example-2 : (Ref. Example-1)
If Tweety is a penguin, it is incorrect to conclude that Tweety flies.

(Incorrect because, in example-1, default rules were applied when case-specific information was not available.)

- All non-monotonic reasoning are concerned with consistency.
- Inconsistency is resolved, by removing the relevant conclusion(s) derived by default rules, as shown in the example below.

Example -3 :

- The truth value (true or false), of propositions such as "Tweety is a bird" accepts default that is normally true, such as "Birds typically fly".

   A conclusion derived was *"Tweety flies"*.

- When an inconsistency is recognized, only the truth value of the last type is changed.

Methods of Reasoning

- Generally there are three kinds of logical reasoning: Deduction, Induction, Abduction.

1. Deduction

Example: "When it rains, the grass gets wet. It rains. Thus, the grass is wet."

- This means in determining the conclusion; it is using rule and its preconditioned to make a conclusion.
- Applying a general principle to a special case.
- Using theory to make predictions
- Usage: Inference engines, Theorem provers, planning.

- Induction

Example: "The grass has been wet every time it has rained. Thus, when it rains, the grass gets wet."

- This means in determining the rule; it is learning the rule after numerous examples of conclusion following the precondition.
- Deriving a general principle from special cases
- From observations to generalizations to knowledge
- Usage: Neural nets, Bayesian nets, Pattern recognition

- Abduction

Example: "When it rains, the grass gets wet. The grass is wet, it must have rained."

- Means determining the precondition; it is using the conclusion and the rule to support that the precondition could explain the conclusion.
- Guessing that some general principle can relate a given pattern of cases
- Extract hypotheses to form a tentative theory
- Usage: Knowledge discovery, Statistical methods, Data mining.

Default Reasoning

- This is a very common form of non-monotonic reasoning. The conclusions are drawn based on what is most likely to be true.
- There are two approaches; both are logic type, to Default reasoning: one is Non-monotonic logic and the other is Default logic.

1. Non-monotonic logic

- It has already been defined. It says, "the truth of a proposition may change when new information (axioms) are added and a logic may be built to allow the statement to be retracted."
- Non-monotonic logic is predicate logic with one extension called modal operator M which means "consistent with everything we know".
- The purpose of M is to allow consistency.

- A way to define consistency with PROLOG notation is :*To show that fact P is true, we attempt to prove ¬P.*
- If we fail we may say that P is consistent since ¬P is false.

Example :
"x : plays_instrument(x) Ù M manage(x) ® jazz_musician(x)

- States that for all x, the x plays an instrument and if the fact that x can manage is consistent with all other knowledge then we can conclude that x is a jazz musician.

2. Default Logic

- Default logic initiates a new inference rule

- Where, A is known as the prerequisite, B as the justification, and C as the consequent.
- Read the above inference rule as: " if A, and if it is consistent with the rest of what is known to assume that B, then conclude that C ".
- The rule says that given the prerequisite, the consequent can be inferred, provided it is consistent with the rest of the data.

Example :
Rule that "birds typically fly" would be represented as,

- Which says, "If x is a bird and the claim that x flies is consistent with what we know, then infer that x flies".
- The idea behind non-monotonic reasoning is to reason with first order logic, and if an inference cannot be obtained then use the set of default rules available within the first order formulation.

CHAPTER SEVEN

STATISTICAL REASONING

Introduction

- We have described several representation techniques that can be used to model belief systems in which, at any given point in time, a particular fact is believed to be true, believed to be false or not considered to be either.
- But for some kinds, it is useful to be able to describe beliefs that are not certain but for which there is some supporting evidence.
- For example, problems that contain genuine randomness. E.g. Card Games
- Problems that could, in principle be modeled using the techniques that we used in uncertainty.
- For such problems, statistical measures may serve a very useful function as summaries of the world; rather than looking for all possible exceptions we can use a numerical summary that tells us how often an exception of some sort can be expected to occur.

- This is useful for dealing with problems where there is randomness and unpredictability (such as in games of chance) and also for dealing with problems where we could, if we had sufficient information, work out exactly what is true.
- To do all this in a principled way requires techniques for probabilistic reasoning.

Statistical Reasoning

Probability & Bayes Theorem

- In probability theory, Bayes' theorem or Bayes' rule describes the probability of an event, based on the prior knowledge of conditions that might be related to the event.
- The Bayes' theorem is expressed in the following formula:

$$P(A|B) = \frac{P(B|A) \cdot P(A)}{P(B)}$$

- Where,

    ○ P(A|B) – the probability of event A occurring, given that event B has occurred
    ○ P(B|A) – the probability of event B occurring, given that event A has occurred
    ○ P(A) – the probability of event A
    ○ P(B) – the probability of event B

- Suppose in a school with 100 students. Out of those 55 students study math (event A), 25 study biology (event B), and 20 study both.
- Here,

  - P(A|B) = probability that a student studies math given that he studies biology
  - P(B|A) = probability that a student studies biology given that he studies math

- Now suppose, if we want to find what is the probability that a student selected randomly studies math given that he studies biology also?
- As per the Condition probability definition:

$$(A \text{ given } B) : ?(?|?) = ?(? \cap ?) / ?(?)$$
$$(B \text{ given } A) : ?(?|?) = ?(? \cap ?) / ?(?)$$

- Applying Bayes' Theorem,

$$?(?|?) = \frac{?(?|?) \cdot ?(?)}{?(?)}$$
$$(?|?) = \frac{(0.20) \cdot (0.55) = 0.8}{(0.55).(0.25)}$$
$$(?|?) = \frac{(0.8) \cdot (0.25) = 0.36}{(0.55)}$$

- Bayes' theorem is used in various disciplines like statistics, medicine, management, different fields of finance, etc.

Certainty Factors & Rule Based Systems

- In this we are trying to describe a practical way of compromising on a pure Bayesian System.
- We will use MYCIN as an example here which uses LISP and acts as an Expert System.
- MYCIN uses the rules to reason Backwards to the clinical data available from its goal of finding significant disease-causing organisms.
- Each rule has a certainty attached to it. Once the identities of the organism are found, it then attempts to select a therapy by which the disease can be treated.
- A certainty factor (CF [h, e])is defined in terms of two components:

1. MB[h, e]- a measure (between 0 and 1) of belief in hypothesis "h" given the evidence "e".

   - MB measures the extent to which the evidence supports the hypothesis.
   - It is zero if the evidence fails to support the hypothesis.

2. MD[h, e]- a measure (between 0 and 1) of disbelief in hypothesis "h" given the evidence "e".

   - MD measures the extent to which the evidence supports the negation of the hypothesis. It is zero if the evidence support the hypothesis.

CF[h, e] = MB[h, e]- MD[h, e]

- Since any particular piece of evidence either supports or denies a Hypothesis (but not both) and since each MYCIN rule corresponds to one piece of evidence (can be compound piece of evidence) a single number suffices for each rule to define both MB and MD and thus the CF.
- The CFs are provided by the experts who write the rules. They reflect the experts'

assessments of the strength of the evidence in support of the Hypothesis.

- At times CFs need to be combined to reflect the operation of multiple pieces of evidence and multiple rules applied to a problem.
- The combining functions should satisfy the following properties :
- Since the order in which evidence is collected is arbitrary, the combining functions should be commutative and associative.

- Until certainty is reached, additional confirming evidence should increase MB and similarly for disconfirming evidence, MD.
- If uncertain inference are chained together, then the result should be less certain that either of the inferences alone.
- By use of CFs we reduce the complexity of a Bayesian reasoning system by making some approximations to the formalism.

Bayesian Networks

- It is an alternative approach to what we did in the previous section.
- The idea is to describe the real world, it is not necessary to use a huge joint probability table in which we list the probabilities of all combinations, because most events are independent of each other, there is no need to consider the interactions between them.
- We will use a more local representation in which we will describe clusters of events that interact.
- Let us consider an example as,

S: sprinkler was on last night W: grass is wet
R: it rained last night

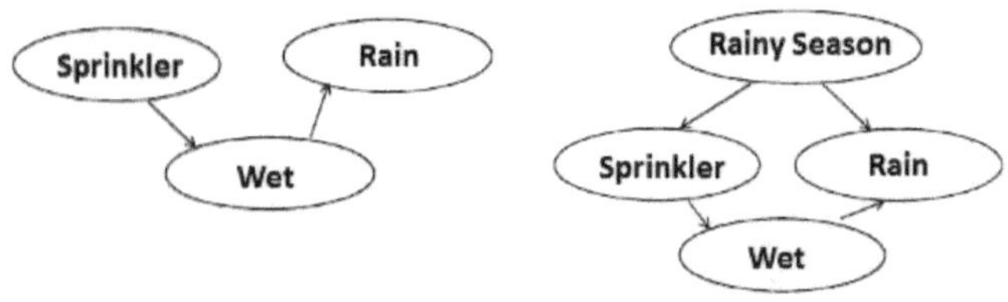

- There are two different ways that propositions can influence the likelihood of each other.

1. The first is that causes influence to the likelihood of their symptoms.

2. The second is that observing a symptom affects the likelihood of all its possible causes.

- The main idea behind the Bayesian network structure is to make a clear distinction between these two kinds of influences.
- The Graph in above figure is known as DAG (Directed A cyclic Graph) that represents causality relationships among the variables.
- However, we need more information. In particular, we need to know, for each value of a parent node, what evidence is provided about the values that the child node can take on.
- We create a probability table for that.
- When the most genuine reasoning does not seem true then we need to use an undirected graph in which the arcs can be used to transmit probabilities in either direction, depending upon where the evidence came from.
- We have to ensure that there is no cycle that exists between the evidences.
- Three algorithms are available for doing these computations
- A message-passing method.
- A cliché triangulation method.
- A variety of stochastic algorithms.
- The message-passing approach is based on the observation that to compute the probability of a node A given what is known about other nodes in the network.
- It is necessary to know three things.

  ◦ The total support arriving at A from its parents.
  ◦ The total support arriving at A from its children.

- ○ The entry in the fixed condition probability matrix that relates A to its causes.

- Cliché triangulation method.

  - ○ Explicit arcs are introduced between pair of nodes that share a common descendent.

- Stochastic Algorithm or Randomized Algorithms

  - ○ The idea is to shield a given node probabilistically from most of the other nodes in the network. These algorithms run faster but may not give correct results.

- Dempster – Shafer Theory
- Till now, we have talked about individual propositions and assign to each of them a single number of the degree of belief that is warranted given the evidence.
- In Dempster-Shafer Theory we consider sets of propositions and assign to each of them an interval in which the degree of belief must lie.
- *[Belief, Plausibility]*
- Belief (denoted as Bel) measures the strength of the evidence in favor of a set of propositions.
- It ranges from 0 (no evidence) to 1 (definite certainty)
- Plausibility (PI) is,
- $PI(s) = 1 - Bel(\neg s)$
- It also ranges from 0 to 1 and measures the extent to which evidence in favor of $\neg s$ leaves room for belief in s.
- In short if we have certain evidence in favor of $(\neg s)$, then Bel(not(s)) will be 1 and Pl(s) will be 0.

- This tells us that the only possible value for Bel(s) is also 0.
- The interval, also tells about the amount of information that we have.
- If we have no evidence we say that the hypothesis is in
- the range of $[0, 1]$.
- As we gain more evidence, this interval can be expected to shrink, and giving confident answers. This is different from Bayesian as in that we would probably begin by distributing the probability among the hypotheses (.33 in case of 3) and we may end up with the same probability at the end, but in Dempster we state that we have no information at the start and everything is in the range of 0 to 1.
- Let's take an example where we have some mutually exclusive hypothesis.
- {Allergy, Flu, Cold, Pneumonia}, The set is denoted by θ.
- We want to attach some measure of belief to elements of θ.
- But all evidences are not directly supportive of individual elements.
- The key function we use here is a Probability Density Function, denoted by m.
- The function m, is not only defined for elements of θ but also all subsets of it.
- The quantity m(p) measures the amount of belief that is currently assigned to exactly to
- the set "p" of hypothesis.
- If θ contains n elements then there are 2^n subsets of θ.
- We must assign m so that the sum of all the m values assigned to subsets of θ is 1.

- At the beginning we have m as under θ = (1.0)
- If we get an evidence of .6 magnitude that the correct diagnosis is in the set {Flu, Cold, Pneu} then,
- **{Flu, Cold, Pneu} = (0.6)**

  $\theta = (0.4)$
- This does not lead us anywhere, we need more information.
- Now to move further, let's consider we have two belief function m1 and m2.
- Let X be the set of subsets of θ to which m1 assigns a nonzero value and let Y be the corresponding set for m2.
- We define m3, as a combination of the m1 and m2 to be,
- $$?_?$$

$$(?) = \sum\nolimits_{?\cap?=?} ?_?(?) \cdot ?_?(?)$$

$$? - \sum\nolimits_{?\cap?=\varnothing} ?_?(?) \cdot ?_?(?)$$

- For example, suppose m1 corresponds to our belief after observing fever:
- m1= { F, C, P} = 0.6

  $\theta = (0.4)$
- suppose m2 corresponds to our belief after observing runny nose:
- m2= { A ,F, C} =0.8

  $\theta = 0.2$
- Then we can compute their combination m3 using the following table.

		{A, F, C}	(0.8)	Θ	(0.2)
{F, C, P}	(0.6)	{F, C}	(0.48)	{F, C, P}	(0.12)
Θ	(0.4)	{A, F, C}	(0.32)	Θ	(0.08)

Fuzzy Logic

- Fuzzy logic is a form of many-valued logic in which the truth values of variables may be any real number between 0 and 1.
- By contrast, in Boolean logic, the truth values of variables may only be the integer values 0 or 1.
- Fuzzy logic has been employed to handle the concept of partial truth, where the truth value may range between completely true and completely false.
- Furthermore, when linguistic variables are used, these degrees may be managed by specific (membership) functions.
- In the standard Boolean definition for tall people are either tall or not and there must be a specific height that defines the boundary.
- Once set membership has been redefined in this way, it is possible to define a reasoning system based on the techniques for combining distributions.
- Such methods have been used in control systems for devices like trains, AC, and washing machines.
- The concepts of Fuzzy Logic are extensively applied in business, finance, aerospace, defense, etc.

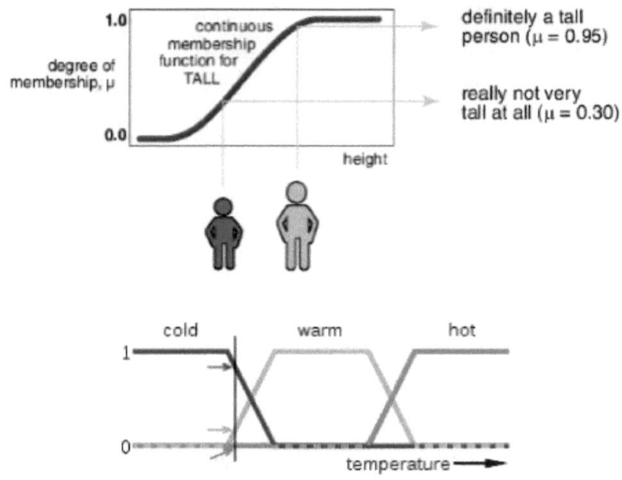

- In above image, the meanings of the expressions cold, warm, and hot are represented by functions mapping a temperature scale.
- A point on that scale has three "truth values"—one for each of the three functions.
- The vertical line in the image represents a particular temperature that the three arrows (truth values) gauge.
- Since the red arrow points to zero, this temperature may be interpreted as "not hot". The orange arrow (pointing at 0.2) may describe it as "slightly warm" and the blue arrow (pointing at 0.8) "fairly cold".

Fuzzy Sets and Membership function

- Fuzzy logic is a set of mathematical principles for knowledge representation based on degrees of membership rather than on crisp membership of classical binary logic.

- Unlike two-valued Boolean logic, fuzzy logic is multi-valued. It deals with degrees of membership.
- The concept of a set is fundamental to mathematics. Crisp set theory is governed by a logic that uses one of only two values: true or false.
- This logic cannot represent vague concepts, and therefore fails to give the answers on the inconsistencies.
- In fuzzy set theory, an element is with a certain degree of membership. Thus, a proposition is not either true or false, but may be partly true (or partly false) to any degree.
- This degree is usually taken as a real number in the interval [0,1].
- The classical example in fuzzy sets is tall men. The elements of the fuzzy set "tall men" are

all men, but their degrees of membership depend on their height.

Name	Height in cm	Degree of Membership	
		Crisp	Fuzzy
John	208	1	1
Tom	181	1	0.8
Bob	152	0	0.0
Mike	198	1	0.9
Billy	158	0	0.4

- In the classical logic, we have a crisp set in which if we ask the question: Is the man tall? Then the tall men are above 180, and not tall men are below 180.

Fuzzy set asks the question: How tall is the man? The tall is partial membership in the fuzzy set, e.g. Mike is 0.9 tall.

CHAPTER EIGHT

WEAK SLOT-AND-FILLER STRUCTURES

Introduction

- Inheritance property can be represented using *isa* and *instance* links.
- Monotonic Inheritance can be performed substantially more efficiently with such structures than with pure logic, and non-monotonic inheritance is also easily supported.
- The reason that makes Inheritance easy is that the knowledge in slot and filler systems is structured as a set of entities and their attributes.
- These structures turn out to be useful as,

  - It indexes assertions by the entities they describe. As a result, retrieving the value for an attribute of an entity is fast.

- ◦ It makes easy to describe properties of relations. To do this in a purely logical system requires higher-order mechanisms.
- ◦ It is a form of object-oriented programming and has the advantages that such systems normally include modularity and ease of viewing by people.

- Here we would describe two views of this kind of structure - Semantic Nets & Frames.

Semantic Nets

- There are different approaches of knowledge representation include semantic net, frames and script.
- The semantic net describes both objects and events.
- In a semantic net, information is represented as a set of nodes connected to each other by a set of labeled arcs, which represents relationships among the nodes.
- It is a directed graph consisting of vertices which represent concepts and edges which represent semantic relations between the concepts.
- It is also known as associative net due to the association of one node with other.
- The main idea is that the meaning of the concept comes from the ways in which it is connected to other concepts.
- We can use inheritance to derive additional relations.

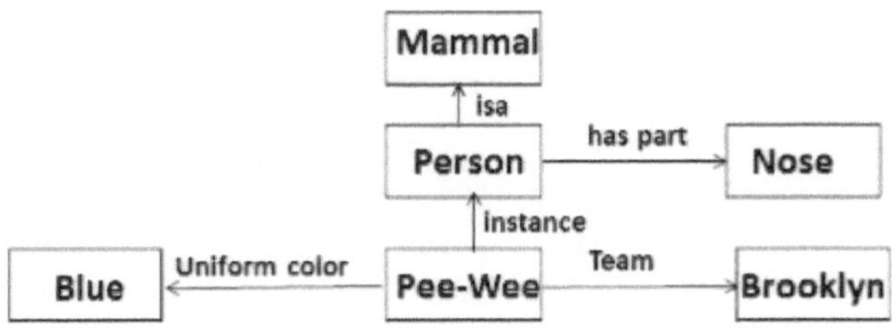

Figure 8.1 A Semantic Network

Intersection Search

- We try to find relationships among objects by spreading activation out from each of two nodes and seeing where the activation meets.
- Using this we can answer the questions like, *what is the relation between India and Blue.*
- It takes advantage of entity based organization of knowledge that slot and filler representation provides.

Representing Non-binary Predicates

- Simple binary predicates like isa(Person, Mammal) can be represented easily by semantic nets but other non-binary predicates can also be represented by using general-purpose predicates such as *isa* and *instance.*
- Three or even more place predicates can also be converted to a binary form by creating one new object representing the entire predicate statement and then introducing binary predicates to describe relationship to this new object.

Example score(Australia, India, 250-275)

- Making important distinctions

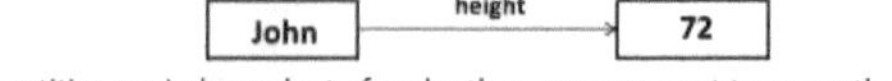

- These entities are independent of each other, now we want to prove that John is taller than Bill then we can represent it by,

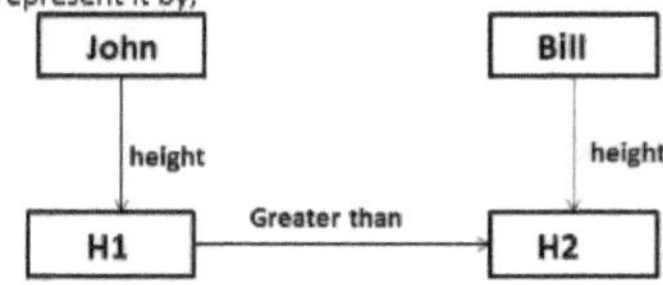

Partitioned Semantic Nets

- If we want to represent simple quantified expressions in semantic nets then it can be done with the help of partitioning the semantic net into a hierarchical set of spaces, each of which corresponds to the scope of one or more variable.
- For example,

The dog bit the mail carrier.

- This is simple and can be easily represented as shown in figure 8.2 (a).
- In this figure d, b and m represent a particular dog, a particular biting and a particular mail

carrier.

- Now suppose we want to represent following fact,

Every dog has bitten a mail carrier.

- To represent this fact, it is necessary to encode the scope of the universally quantified variable x. this can be done using partitioning as shown in figure 8.2 (b).
- The node g is given for the assertion. Node g is an instance of the special case GS of general statements about the world.
- very element of GS has at least two attributes: a form and one or more connections.

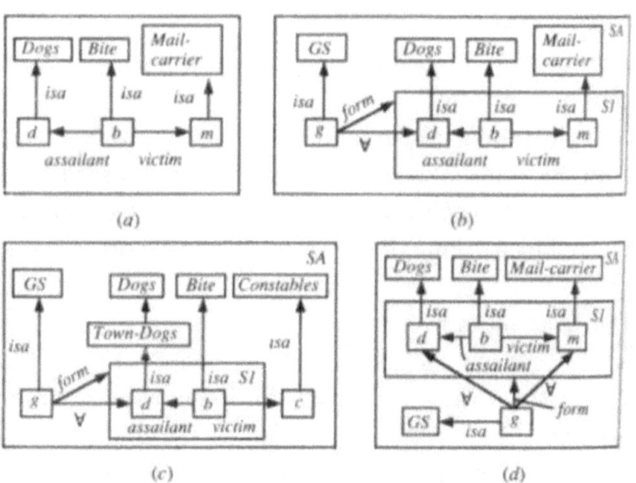

(a)   (b)

(c)   (d)

Figure 8.2 Partitioned Semantic Net

Figure 8.2 (c) represents the similar sentences,

Every dog in town has bitten the constable.

Figure 8.2 (d) represents,

Every dog has bitten every mail carrier.

Evolution of Frames

- As seen in the previous example, there are certain problems which are difficult to solve with Semantic Nets.
- Although there is no clear distinction between a semantic net and frame system, but more structured the system is, more likely it is to be termed as a frame system.
- A frame is a collection of attributes (called slots) and associated values that describe some entities in the world. Sometimes a frame describes an entity in some absolute sense;
- Sometimes it represents the entity from a particular point of view only.
- A single frame taken alone is rarely useful; we build frame systems out of collections of frames that are connected to each other by virtue of the fact that the value of an attribute of one frame may be another frame.

Frames as Sets and Instances

- The set theory is a good basis for understanding frame systems.
- Each frame represents either a class (a set) or an instance (an element of class)
- Both *isa* and *instance* relations have inverse attributes, which we call subclasses & all- instances.

- As a class represents a set, there are 2 kinds of attributes that can be associated with it.

1. Its own attributes &
2. Attributes that are to be inherited by each element of the set.

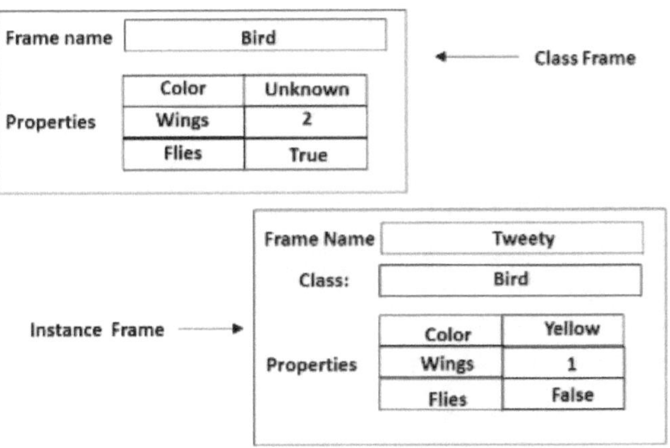

Frames as Sets and Instances

3. Sometimes, the difference between a set and an individual instance may not be clear.
4. Example: Team India is an instance of class of Cricket Teams and can also be thought of as set of players.
5. Now the problem is if we present Team India as a sub class of Cricket teams, then Indian players automatically become part of all the teams, which is not true.
6. So, we can make Team India a sub class of class called Cricket Players.

7. To do this we need to differentiate between regular classes and meta-classes.

8. Regular Classes are those whose elements are individual entities whereas Meta-classes are those special classes whose elements are themselves classes.

9. The most basic meta-class is the class *CLASS*.

10. It represents the set of all classes.

11. All classes are instances of it, either directly or through one of its subclasses.

12. The class *CLASS* introduces the attribute cardinality, which is to be inherited by all instances of CLASS. Cardinality stands for number.

13. Other ways of Relating Classes to Each Other

14. We have discussed that a class1 can be a subset of class2.

15. If Class2 is a meta-class then Class1 can be an instance of Class2.

16. Another way is ***mutually-disjoint-with*** relationship, which relates a class to one or more other classes that are guaranteed to have no elements in common with it.

17. Another one is, ***is-covered-by*** which relates a class to a set of subclasses, the union of which is equal to it.

18. If a class is-covered-by a set S of mutually disjoint classes, then S is called a partition of the class.

19. Slots as Full-Fledged Objects (Frames)

20. Till now we have used attributes as slots, but now we will represent attributes explicitly and describe their properties.

21. Some of the properties we would like to be able to represent and use in reasoning include,

- ○ The class to which the attribute can be attached.
- ○ Constraints on either the type or the value of the attribute.
- ○ A default value for the attribute. Rules for inheriting values for the attribute.
- ○ To be able to represent these attributes of attributes, we need to describe attributes (slots) as frames.
- ○ These frames will be organized into an *isa* hierarchy, just as any other frames are, and that hierarchy can then be used to support inheritance of values for attributes of slots.
- ○ Now let us formalize what is a slot. A slot here is about a relation.
- ○ It maps from elements of its domain (the classes for which it makes sense) to elements of its range (its possible values).
- ○ A relation is a set of ordered pairs.
- ○ Thus it makes sense to say that relation R1 is a subset of another relation R2.
- ○ In that case R1 is a specialization of R2. Since a slot is a set, the set of all slots, which we will call SLOT, is a meta-class.
- ○ Its instances are slots, which may have sub slots.

Frame Example

- In this example, the frames Person, Adult-Male, ML-Baseball-Player (corresponding to major league baseball players), Pitcher, and ML-Baseball-Team (for major league baseball team) are all classes.

```
Person
    isa :                        Mammal
    cardinality :                6,000,000,000
    * handed :                   Right
Adult-Male
    isa :                        Person
    cardinality :                2,000,000,000
    * height :                   5-10
ML-Baseball-Player
    isa :                        Adult-Male
    cardinality :                624
    *height :                    6-1
    * bats :                     equal to handed
    * batting-average :          .252
    * team :
    * uniform-color :
Fielder
    isa :                        ML-Baseball-Player
    cardinality :                376
    *batting-average :           .262
Pee-Wee-Reese
    instance :                   Fielder
    height :                     5-10
    bats :                       Right
    batting-average :            .309
    team :                       Brooklyn-Dodgers
    uniform-color :              Blue
ML-Baseball-Team
    isa:                         Team
    cardinality :                26
    * team-size :                24
    * manager :
Brooklyn-Dodgers
    instance :                   ML-Baseball-Team
    team-size :                  24
    manager :                    Leo-Durocher
    players :                    {Pee-Wee-Reese,...}
```

- The frames Pee-Wee-Reese and Brooklyn-Dodgers are instances.
- The *isa* relation that we have been using without a precise definition is in fact the subset relation. The set of adult males is a subset of the set of people.
- The set of major league baseball players is a subset of the set of adult males, and so forth.
- Our instance relation corresponds to the relation element-of Pee Wee Reese is an element of the set of fielders.
- Thus he is also an element of all of the supersets of fielders, including major league baseball players and people. The transitivity of *isa* follows directly from the transitivity of the subset relation.
- Both the isa and instance relations have inverse attributes, which we call subclasses and all- instances.
- Because a class represents a set, there are two kinds of attributes that can be associated with it.
- Some attributes are about the set itself, and some attributes are to be inherited by each element of the set.
- We indicate the difference between these two by prefixing the latter with an asterisk (*).
- For example, consider the class ML-Baseball-Player, we have shown only two properties of it as a set: It is a subset of the set of adult males. And it has cardinality 624.
- We have listed five properties that all major league baseball players have (height, bats, batting-average, team, and uniform-color), and we have specified default values for the first three of them.
- By providing both kinds of slots, we allow a both class to define a set of objects and to describe a prototypical object of the set.

- Frames are useful for representing objects that are typical to stereotypical situations.
- The situation like structure of complex physical objects, visual scenes, etc.
- A commonsense knowledge can be represented using default values if no other value exits. Commonsense is generally used in the absence of specific knowledge.

CHAPTER NINE

STRONG SLOT-AND-FILLER STRUCTURES

Introduction

- The main problem with semantic networks and frames is that they lack formality; there is no specific guideline on how to use the representations.
- In frame when things change, we need to modify all frames that are relevant – this can be time consuming.
- Strong slot and filler structures typically represent links between objects according to more rigid rules, specific notions of what types of object and relations between them are provided and represent knowledge about common situations.
- We have types of strong slot and filler structures:

1. Conceptual Dependency (CD)

2. Scripts
3. Cyc

1. Conceptual Dependency (CD)

- Conceptual Dependency is originally developed to represent knowledge acquired from natural language input.
- The goals of this theory are:

  - To help in the drawing of inference from sentences.
  - To be independent of the words used in the original input.
  - That is to say: For any 2 (or more) sentences that are identical in meaning there should be only one representation of that meaning.

- It has been used by many programs that portend to understand English (MARGIE, SAM, PAM).
- Conceptual Dependency (CD) provides:

  - A structure into which nodes representing information can be placed.
  - A specific set of primitives.
  - A given level of granularity.

- Sentences are represented as a series of diagrams depicting actions using both abstract and real physical situations.

  - The agent and the objects are represented.

- ◦ The actions are built up from a set of primitive acts which can be modified by tense.

- CD is based upon events and actions. Every event (if applicable) has:

  - ◦ an ACTOR
  - ◦ an ACTION performed by the Actor
  - ◦ an OBJECT that the action performs on
  - ◦ a DIRECTION in which that action is oriented

- These are represented as slots and fillers. In English sentences, many of these attributes are left out.

A Simple Conceptual Dependency Representation

- For the sentences, "I gave a book to the man" CD representation is as follows:

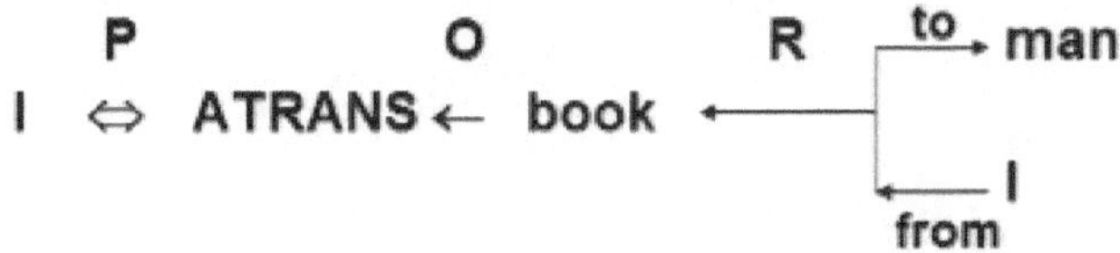

- Where the symbols have the following meaning.
- Arrows indicate directions of dependency.
- Double arrow indicates two way link between actor and action.
- O -- for the object case relation
- R – for the recipient case relation
- P – for past tense

- D - destination
- EXPEL Expulsion of something from the body of an animal (e.g. cry) MTRANS Transfer of mental information (e.g. tell)

  MBUILD Building new information out of old (e.g decide) SPEAK Producing of sounds (e.g. say)

  ATTEND Focusing of a sense organ toward a stimulus (e.g. listen)
- There are four conceptual categories. These are, ACT Actions {one of the CD primitives} PP Objects {picture producers}
- AA Modifiers of actions {action aiders} PA Modifiers of PP's {picture aiders}

  Primitive Acts of CD theory

  ATRANS Transfer of an abstract relationship (i.e. give)

  PTRANS Transfer of the physical location of an object (e.g., go) PROPEL Application of physical force to an object (e.g. push) MOVE Movement of a body part by its owner (e.g. kick) GRASP Grasping of an object by an action (e.g. throw) INGEST Ingesting of an object by an animal (e.g. eat)
- The primitives are used to define conceptual dependency relationships or Conceptual syntax rules.

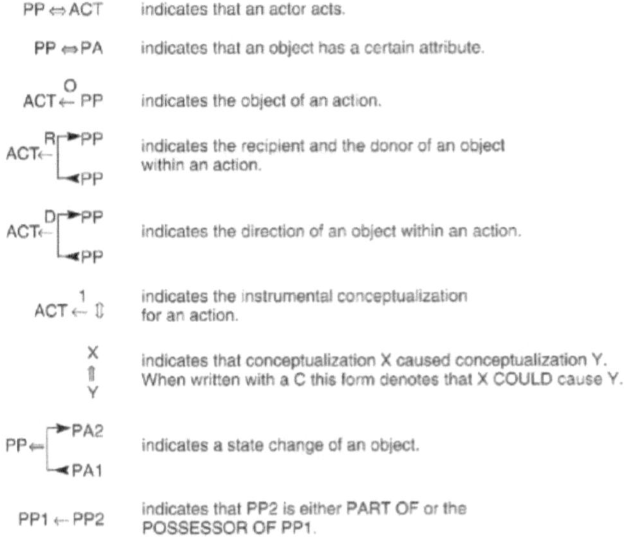

- Advantages of CD:
- Using these primitives involves fewer inference rules.
- Many inference rules are already represented in CD structure.
- The holes in the initial structure help to focus on the points still to be established.
- Disadvantages of CD:

  - It must be activated based on its significance.
  - If the topic is important, then the script should be opened.
  - If a topic is just mentioned, then a pointer to that script could be held.

- For example, given "John enjoyed the play in theater", a script "Play in Theater" suggested

- above is invoked.

  - All implicit questions can be answered correctly.
  - Here the significance of this script is high.

    ◦ Did john go to theater?
    ◦ Did he buy ticket?
    ◦ Did he have money?

  - If we have a sentence like "John went to theater to pick his daughter", then invoking this

- script will lead to many wrong answers.

    ◦ Here significance of the script theater is less.

  - Getting significance from the story is not straightforward. However, some heuristics can be
-     applied to get the value.

- CYC
- What is CYC?
- An ambitious attempt to form a very large knowledge base aimed at capturing commonsense reasoning.
- Initial goals to capture knowledge from a hundred randomly selected articles in the EnCYClopedia Britannica.
- Both Implicit and Explicit knowledge encoded.
- Emphasis on study of underlying information (assumed by the authors but not needed to tell to the readers.

- Example: Suppose we read that Wellington learned of Napoleon's death
- Then we (humans) can conclude Napoleon never new that Wellington had died.
- How do we do this?
- We require special implicit knowledge or commonsense such as:
- We only die once.
- You stay dead.
- You cannot learn of anything when dead.
- Time cannot go backwards.
- Why build large knowledge bases:
- Brittleness

  - Specialised knowledge bases are brittle. Hard to encode new situations and non-graceful degradation in performance. Commonsense based knowledge bases should have a firmer foundation.

- Form and Content

  - Knowledge representation may not be suitable for AI. Commonsense strategies could point out where difficulties in content may affect the form.

- Shared Knowledge

  - Should allow greater communication among systems with common bases and assumptions.

- How is CYC coded?
- By hand.
- Special CYCL language:

- LISP like.
- Frame based
- Multiple inheritance
- Slots are fully fledged objects.
- Generalized inheritance -- any link not just *isa* and
- *instance.*
- Knowledge must be decomposed into fairly low level primitives.
- Impossible or difficult to find correct set of primitives.
- A lot of inference may still be required.
- Representations can be complex even for relatively simple actions.
- Consider: Dave bet Frank five pounds that Wales would win the Rugby World Cup.
- Complex representations require a lot of storage
- Scripts

  - A script is a structure that prescribes a set of circumstances which could be expected to follow on from one another.
  - It is similar to a thought sequence or a chain of situations which could be anticipated.
  - It could be considered to consist of a number of slots or frames but with more specialized roles.
  - Scripts are beneficial because:

    - Events tend to occur in known runs or patterns.
    - Causal relationships between events exist.
    - Entry conditions exist which allow an event to take place
    - Prerequisites exist upon events taking place. E.g. when a student progresses through a degree
  - scheme or when a purchaser buys a house.

Script Components

- Each script contains the following main components.

  - Entry Conditions: Must be satisfied before events in the script can occur.
  - Results: Conditions that will be true after events in script occur.
  - Props: Slots representing objects involved in the events.
  - Roles: Persons involved in the events.
  - Track: Specific variation on more general pattern in the script. Different tracks may share many components of the same script but not all.
  - Scenes: The sequence of events that occur. Events are represented in conceptual dependency form.

- Advantages / Disadvantages of Script

- Advantages

  - Capable of predicting implicit events
  - Single coherent interpretation may be build up from a collection of observations.

- Disadvantage

  - More specific (inflexible) and less general than frames.
  - Not suitable to represent all kinds of knowledge.

- To deal with inflexibility, smaller modules called memory organization packets (MOP) can be

- combined in a way that is appropriate for the situation.

CHAPTER TEN

GAME PLAYING

Introduction to Game playing

- Charles Babbage, the nineteenth century computer architect thought about programming his analytical engine to play chess and later of building a machine to play tic-tac-toe.
- There are two reasons that games appeared to be a good domain.

1. They provide a structured task in which it is very easy to measure success or failure.
2. They are easily solvable by straightforward search from the starting state to a winning position.

- The first is true is for all games bust the second is not true for all, except simplest games.
- For example consider chess.
- The average branching factor is around 35. In an average game, each player might make 50.

- So in order to examine the complete game tree, we would have to examine 35^{100} positions.
- Thus it is clear that a simple search is not able to select even its first move during the lifetime of its opponent.
- It is clear that to improve the effectiveness of a search based problem solving program two things can be done.

1. Improve the generate procedure so that only good moves are generated.
2. Improve the test procedure so that the best move will be recognized and explored first.

- If we use legal-move generator then the test procedure will have to look at each of them, because the test procedure must look at so many possibilities, it must be fast.
- Instead of legal-move generator we can use plausible-move generator in which only some small numbers of promising moves are generated.
- As the number of legal available moves increases it becomes increasingly important in applying heuristics to select only those moves that seem more promising.
- The performance of overall system can be improved by adding heuristic knowledge into both the generator and the tester.
- In game playing, a goal state is one in which we win but the game like chess, it is not possible, even we have good plausible move generator.
- The depth of the resulting tree or graph and its branching factor is too great.

- It is possible to search tree only ten or twenty moves deep then in order to choose the best move, the resulting board positions must be compared to discover which is most advantageous.
- This is done using static evolution function, which uses whatever information it has to evaluate individual board position by estimating how likely they are to lead eventually to a win.
- Its function is similar to that of the heuristic function h' in the A* algorithm: in the absence

of complete information, choose the most promising position.

The MINIMAX search procedure

- The minimax search is a depth first and depth limited procedure.
- The idea is to start at the current position and use the plausible-move generator to generate the set of possible successor positions.
- Now we can apply the static evolution function to those positions and simply choose the best one.
- After doing so, we can back that value up to the starting position to represent our evolution of it.
- Here we assume that static evolution function returns larger values to indicate good situations for us.
- So our goal is to maximize the value of the static evaluation function of the next board position.
- The opponents' goal is to minimize the value of the static evaluation function.

- *The alternation of maximizing and minimizing at alternate ply when evaluations are to be pushed back up corresponds to the opposing strategies of the two players is called MINIMAX.*
- It is recursive procedure that depends on two procedures

  ○ MOVEGEN(position, player)— The plausible-move generator, which returns a list of nodes representing the moves that can be made by Player in Position.
  ○ STATIC(position, player)-- static evaluation function, which returns a number representing the goodness of Position from the standpoint of Player.

- With any recursive program, we need to decide when recursive procedure should stop.
- There are variety of factors that may influence the decision they are,

  ○ Has one side won?
  ○ How many ply have we already explored? Or how much time is left?
  ○ How stable is the configuration?

- We use DEEP-ENOUGH which is assumed to evaluate all of these factors and to return TRUE if the search should be stopped at the current level and FALSE otherwise.
- It takes two parameters, position and depth, it will ignore its position parameter and simply return TRUE if its depth parameter exceeds a constant cut off value.

- One problem that arises in defining MINIMAX as a recursive procedure is that it needs to return not one but two results.

  - The backed-up value of the path it chooses.
  - The path itself. We return the entire path even though probably only the first element, representing the best move from the current position, is actually needed.

    - We assume that MINIMAX returns a structure containing both results and we have two functions, VALUE and PATH that extract the separate components.
    - Initially, It takes three parameters, a board position, the current depth of the search, and the player to move,

- MINIMAX(current,0,player-one) If player –one is to move
- MINIMAX(current,0,player-two) If player –two is to move

Algorithm: MINIMAX(position, depth, player)

1. If DEEP-ENOUGH(Position, Depth), then return the structure VALUE = STATIC(Position, Player);

   PATH = nil

   This indicates that there is no path from this node and that its value is that determined by the static evaluation function

1. Otherwise, generate one more ply of the tree by calling the function MOVE-GEN (Position Player) and setting SUCCESSORS to the list it returns.
2. If SUCCESSORS is empty, then there are no moves to be made, so return the same structure that would have been returned if DEEP-ENOUGH had returned true.
3. If SUCCESSORS is not empty, then examine each element in turn and keep track of the best one. This is done as follows.

Initialize BEST-SCORE to the minimum value that STATIC can return. It will be updated to reflect the best score that can be achieved by an element of SUCCESSORS.

For each element SUCC of SUCCESSORS, do the following:

a. Set RESULT-SUCC to **MlNIMAX(SUCC, Depth + 1, OPPOSITE(Player))**.

This recursive call to MINIMAX will actually carry out the exploration of SUCC

b. Set NEW-VALUE to - VALUE (RESULT-SUCC). This will cause it to reflect the merits of the position from the opposite perspective from that of the next lower level

c. If NEW-VALUE > BEST-SCORE, then we have found a successor that is better than any that have been examined so far. Record this by doing the following:

    i. Set BEST-SCORE to NEW-VALUE
    ii. The best known path is now from CURRENT to SUCC and then on to the appropriate path down

from SUCC as determined by the recursive call to MINIMAX. So set BEST-PATH to the result of attaching SUCC to the front of PATH (RESULT-SUCC).

5. Now that all the successors have been examined, we know the value of Position as well as which path to take from it. So return the structure

VALUE = BEST-SCORE PATH = BEST-PATH

- When the initial call to MINIMAX returns, the best move from CURRENT is the first element on PATH. Performance can be improved significantly with a few refinements.

Example

- We use static evaluation function that returns value ranging from -10 to 10, with 10 indicating a win for us,-10 indicating win for opponent, 0 indicating an even match.
- As shown in fig 10.1, we move to B. Backing B's value up to A, we can conclude that A's value is 8.

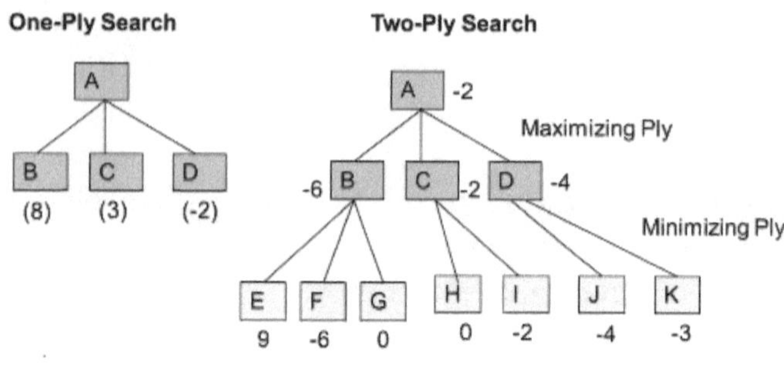

Backing up the values of a Two-Ply Search

- But since we know that the static evaluation function is not completely accurate, we would like to carry the search farther ahead than one ply.
- After one move the situation would appear to be very good, but if we move ahead, situation may not be favorable.
- We first apply plausible move generator, generating a set of successor positions for each position, then we apply static evolution function to each of these position shown in fig 10.1.
- But now we must take into account that the opponent gets to choose which successor moves minimize the ply.
- This mean that if we make move B, the actual position in which we end is -6, because opponent selects it, also there is an E which is very good for us but opponent task is to minimize play shown in the figure.

- The minimum value was chosen and backed up. At the level representing our choice, the maximum value was chosen.
- The process can be repeated as many ply as time allows and more accurate evaluations that are produced can be used to choose the correct move at the top level.
- The alternation of maximizing and minimizing at alternate ply when evaluations are being pushed back up corresponds to the opposing strategies of the two players.
- This method is called **Minimax.**

Adding alpha – beta cutoffs

- Minimax procedure is depth first process. One path is explored as far as time allows, the

static evolution function is applied to the game positions at the last step of the path.

- The efficiency of the depth first search can be improved by branch and bound technique in which partial solutions that are clearly worse than known solutions can be abandoned early.
- It is necessary to modify the branch and bound strategy to include two bounds, one for each of the players.
- This modified strategy is called alpha–beta pruning.
- It requires to maintain of two threshold values, one representing a lower bound on that a maximizing

node may ultimately be assigned (we call this alpha).

- And another representing an upper bound on the value that a minimizing node may be assigned (this we call beta).
- Each level must receive both the values, one to use and one to pass down for the next level to use.
- The MINIMAX procedure as it stands does not need to treat maximizing and minimizing levels differently since it simply negates evaluation each time it changes levels.
- Instead of referring to alpha and beta, MINIMAX uses two values, USE-THRESH and PASS- THRESH.
- USE-THRESH is used to compute cutoffs. PASS-THRESH is passed to next level as its USE- THRESH.
- USE-THRESH must also be passed to the next level, but it will be passed as PASS-THRESH so that it can be passed to third level down as USE-THRESH again, and so forth.
- Just as values had to be negated each time they were passed across levels.
- Still there are no difference between the code required at maximizing levels and that required at minimizing levels.
- PASS-THRESH should always be the maximum of the value it inherits from above and the best move found at its level.
- If PASS-THRESH is updated the new value should be propagated both down to lower levels and back up to higher ones so that it always reflect the best move found anywhere in the tree.
- The MINIMAX-A-B requires five arguments, position, depth, player, Use-thresh, and pass- Thresh.

- MINIMAX-A-B(current,0,player-one,maximum value static can compute, minimum value static can compute)

Algorithm: MINIMAX-A-B(Position, depth, player, use-thresh, pass-thresh)

1. If DEEP-ENOUGH(Position, Depth), then return the structure VALUE = STATIC(Position, Player);

PATH = nil

1. Otherwise, generate one more ply of the tree by calling the function MOVE- GEN(Position, Player) and setting SUCCESSORS to the list it returns.
2. If SUCCESSORS is empty, there are no moves to be made; return the same structure that

would have been returned if DEEP-ENOUGH had returned TRUE.

4. If SUCCESSORS is not empty, then go through it, examining each element and keeping track of the best one. This is done as follows.

For each element SUCC of SUCCESSOR:

a. Set RESULT-SUCC to

MINIMAX-A-B(SUCC, Depth + 1, OPPOSITE(Player), —Pass-Thresh, —Use-Thresh).

b. Set NEW-VALUE to —VALUE (RESULT-SUCC).

c. If NEW-VALUE > Pass-Thresh, then we have found a successor that is better than any that have been examined so far. Record this by doing the following.

   i. Set Pass-Thresh to NEW-VALUE.
   ii. The best known path is now from CURRENT to SUCC and then on to the appropriate path from SUCC as determined by the recursive calls to MINIMAX-A-B. So set BEST-PATH to the result of attaching SUCC to the front of PATH (RESULT-SUCC).

d. If Pass-Thresh Is not better then Use-Thresh, then we should stop examining this branch. But both thresholds and value been inverted. So if Pass-Thresh>=Use- Thresh, then return immediately with the value.

5. Return the structure VALUE=pass-Thresh PATH=BEST-PATH

Example

- To see how the alpha-beta procedure works, consider the example shown in Fig below.
- After examining node F, we know that the opponent is guaranteed a score of -5 or less at C (since the opponent is the minimizing player).
- But we also know that we are guaranteed a score of 3 or greater at node A, which we can achieve if we move to B.
- Any other move that produces a score of less than 3 is worse than the move to B.

- After examining only F, we are sure that a move to C is worse Maximizing ply (it will be less than or equal to -5) regardless of the score of node G.
- So we need not to explore node G.
- So not only one node but if we were exploring this tree to six ply, then we would have eliminated not a single node but an entire tree three ply deep.

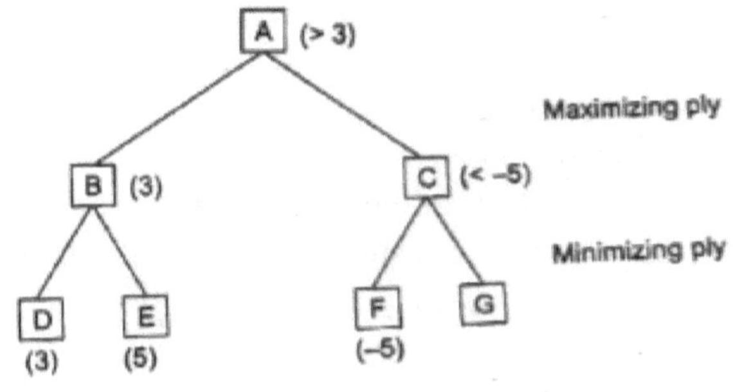

- To see how the two thresholds, alpha and beta, can both be used, consider the example shown in Fig. 10.2.
- The entire sub tree headed by B is searched and we discover that at A, we can accept a score of at least 3.
- When this alpha value is passed down to F, it will enable us to skip the exploration of L let's

see how.

- After K is examined, we see that I is guaranteed a maximum score of 0, which means that F is

guaranteed a minimum of 0.
- But this is less than alpha's value of 3.
- Because we can get score of 3 by moving to B rather then moving to I.
- Now we examined J and we yield 5 because it is grater than 0.
- Now this value becomes the value of beta at node C.
- It indicates that C is guaranteed to get a 5 or less.
- Now we must expand G, first M is examined and it has a value 7 which is passed to G as the tentative value. But now 7 is compared to beta (5).
- It is greater and the player whose turn it is at C is trying to minimize.
- So player will not choose G which would lead to a score of at least 7, since there is an alternative move to F which will lead to a score of 5.

So it is not necessary to explore any of other branches of G.

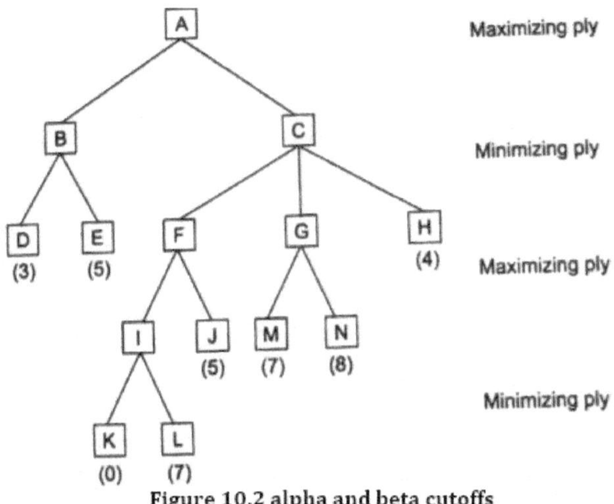

Figure 10.2 alpha and beta cutoffs

Enter Caption

Dr. Ajay Kumar Phulre
Associate Professor (CSE)
Parul Institute of Technology
Parul University Vadodara , Gujarat
Mr. Rahul Sharma
Assitant Professor (CSE)
Parul Institute of Technology
Parul University Vadodara , Gujarat
Mr. Rahul Anjana
Assitant Professor (CSE)
Parul Institute of Technology
Parul University Vadodara , Gujarat
Mr. Chour Singh Rajpoot
Assitant Professor (CSE)
Parul Institute of Technology
Parul University Vadodara , Gujarat

www.ingramcontent.com/pod-product-compliance
Lightning Source LLC
Chambersburg PA
CBHW031627170726
47990CB00017B/393